S. Hrg. 112–490

THE FUTURE OF INTERNET GAMING: WHAT'S AT STAKE FOR TRIBES?

HEARING

BEFORE THE

COMMITTEE ON INDIAN AFFAIRS
UNITED STATES SENATE

ONE HUNDRED TWELFTH CONGRESS

FIRST SESSION

NOVEMBER 17, 2011

Printed for the use of the Committee on Indian Affairs

U.S. GOVERNMENT PRINTING OFFICE

75–092 PDF   WASHINGTON : 2012

For sale by the Superintendent of Documents, U.S. Government Printing Office
Internet: bookstore.gpo.gov   Phone: toll free (866) 512–1800; DC area (202) 512–1800
Fax: (202) 512–2104   Mail: Stop IDCC, Washington, DC 20402–0001

CONTENTS

THE FUTURE OF INTERNET GAMING: WHAT'S AT STAKE FOR TRIBES?

THURSDAY, NOVEMBER 17, 2011

U.S. SENATE,
COMMITTEE ON INDIAN AFFAIRS,
Washington, DC.

The Committee met, pursuant to notice, at 2:15 p.m. in room 628, Dirksen Senate Office Building, Hon. Daniel K. Akaka, Chairman of the Committee, presiding.

OPENING STATEMENT OF HON. DANIEL K. AKAKA, U.S. SENATOR FROM HAWAII

The CHAIRMAN. Thank you, everyone. Thank you for being here. For me, this is a joyous occasion, to see my friend, Al D'Amato. And we have some things that we can talk about in the past that we are affected with, so it is so good to see him. I feel so great that he looks really well. Maybe I shouldn't say he looks better than he did before.

[Laughter.]

The CHAIRMAN. But it is good to have all of you here at this hearing. Senator Barrasso will be here, but I will begin.

The Committee will come to order. Aloha and welcome to all of you, to this Committee's oversight hearing on The Future of Internet Gaming: What's at Stake for Tribes?

Today's hearing will focus on Tribal concerns and priorities related to Internet gaming. Although there is no legislation before the Committee right now, one thing that we are all well aware of is the need for additional revenue sources at the Federal level.

The discussion surrounding the potential Internet gaming legislation has only increased as Congress looks at the Super Committee to find revenue sources and Congress looks to create jobs and economic development opportunities across the United States. And we are really busy on that.

Since the enactment of the Indian Gaming Regulatory Act, Indian gaming has grown to a $26 billion industry. As you can see in the charts that we have here today, in total Indian gaming makes up approximately 43 percent of the entire commercial gaming industry in the United States. That is why it is critical that the Committee explore this issue to find out what it would mean for Tribes and their traditional Indian gaming facilities. We must make sure that the unique circumstances surrounding Tribal sovereignty are maintained in any legislation. We must also enable Tribes to fully participate, so Tribes are on equal footing with their counterparts in the commercial gaming industry, should any legislation be considered.

[The information referred to follows:]

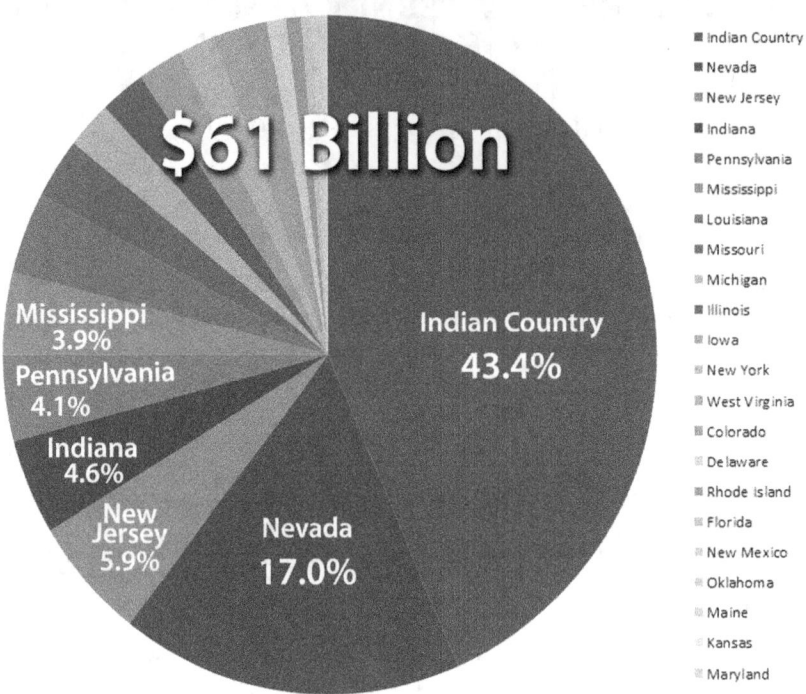

Commercial Gaming Revenue 2010

$61 Billion

Indian Country 43.4%

Nevada 17.0%

New Jersey 5.9%

Indiana 4.6%

Pennsylvania 4.1%

Mississippi 3.9%

- Indian Country
- Nevada
- New Jersey
- Indiana
- Pennsylvania
- Mississippi
- Louisiana
- Missouri
- Michigan
- Illinois
- Iowa
- New York
- West Virginia
- Colorado
- Delaware
- Rhode Island
- Florida
- New Mexico
- Oklahoma
- Maine
- Kansas
- Maryland

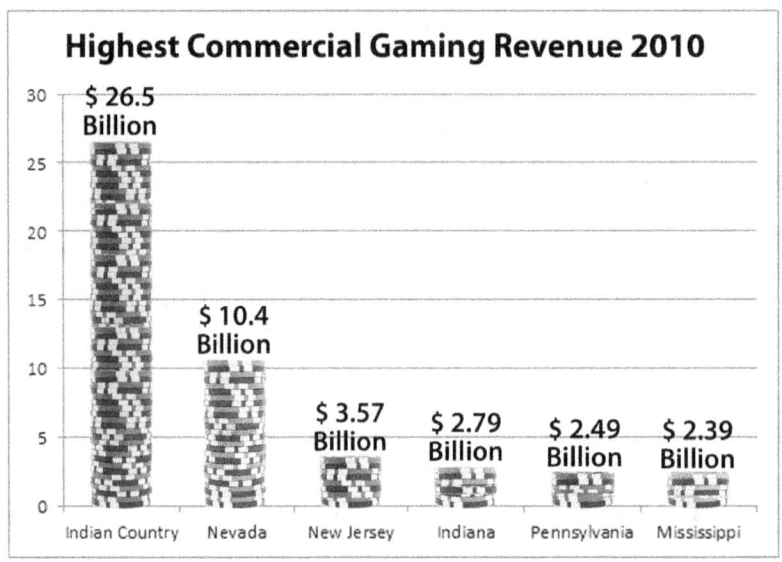

Highest Commercial Gaming Revenue 2010

Indian Country	$ 26.5 Billion
Nevada	$ 10.4 Billion
New Jersey	$ 3.57 Billion
Indiana	$ 2.79 Billion
Pennsylvania	$ 2.49 Billion
Mississippi	$ 2.39 Billion

I know this hearing has created a lot of interest. I would encourage any interested parties to submit comments or written testimony for the record. The hearing record will remain open for two weeks from today.

With that, I would like to welcome our first guest to the table, but before I do that, I want to ask Senator Franken for any remarks he may have.

STATEMENT OF HON. AL FRANKEN,
U.S. SENATOR FROM MINNESOTA

Senator FRANKEN. Thank you. Thank you, Mr. Chairman, first for convening this important hearing and for allowing me to make this opening statement.

As we all know, gaming has been an incredibly powerful economic tool for Tribes. Gaming has brought much-needed revenue and jobs to Indian Country and has allowed Tribes to invest in their communities. I have seen first-hand the positive impacts that Indian gaming has in my home State of Minnesota. Just last week I visited the Mille Lacs Band of the Ojibwa, which uses revenue from its two casinos to fund health clinics, an assisted living facility, a school, a housing program, police department, and a wastewater treatment facility. Mille Lacs has also been able to invest in a number of businesses and runs a small business development program to support members who want to start their own businesses.

Any changes to current gaming laws must take into account the special place the Tribes hold in the gaming industry, both to respect Tribal sovereignty and out of economic fairness. If Congress considers legislation to legalize Internet gaming, although I am not sure about Internet gaming, it seems to me a good way that someone can lose their home in their home. Nevertheless, if Congress considers legislation to legalize Internet gambling, it is vitally important that Tribes are consulted in every step of the process. This hearing is an important first step.

So thank you to all the witnesses that are appearing today, and I look forward to hearing your testimony. Mr. Chairman, thank you very much.

The CHAIRMAN. Thank you very much, Senator Franken.

Our first witness today is Mr. Larry Roberts, who is General Counsel at the National Indian Gaming Commission. Mr. Roberts, thank you so much for being here, and please proceed with your remarks.

STATEMENT OF LAWRENCE S. ROBERTS, GENERAL COUNSEL,
NATIONAL INDIAN GAMING COMMISSION

Mr. ROBERTS. Chairman Akaka, Vice Chairman Barrasso, Senator Franken, members of the Committee, I want to begin by thanking you for inviting the Commission to testify today. My name is Lawrence Roberts and I am a member of the Oneida Nation of Wisconsin. It is an honor to appear before you today to testify in my capacity as General Counsel for the National Indian Gaming Commission.

Today I will provide a brief overview of the Commission's history as well as the current size and location of NIGC offices today. This overview will hopefully prove to be helpful as the Committee proceeds with its hearing.

In 1988, the Indian Gaming Regulatory Act established the National Indian Gaming Commission, a Federal civil regulatory agency. Mr. Anthony Hope, the first Chairman of the NIGC, started at the Commission in the spring of 1990, more than a year and a half after the enactment of IGRA. The second Commissioner, Mr. Joel Frank, Senior, was sworn into office in the fall of 1990, and a third Commissioner, Ms. Jana McKeag, joined the Commission almost a year after the Chairman in 1991.

In these early days, NIGC overcame common hurdles of a new agency before becoming operational, such as securing office space, hiring staff, and promulgating initial regulations.

The agency proposed its first regulations on May 29th, 1991, approximately a year into Chairman Hope's tenure. The first set of regulations concerned the collection of fees. Since NIGC is now entirely funded by Tribal fees assessed on gaming operations, promulgation of these regulations was a top priority and critical to the Commission. The fee regulations were finalized on August 15th, 1991, nearly three years after the enactment of IGRA.

The fee regulations were followed by regulations addressing other statutory duties of the Commission, such as approval of gaming ordinances, approval of management contracts and compliance and enforcement procedures. These and other regulations became effective on February 22nd, 1993. Thus, it was not until 1993 that NIGC began to fully carry out its responsibilities under IGRA. The delay in promulgating regulations governing the approval of ordinances and management contracts may have slowed the entry of Tribes into the gaming arena. During this interim period, the Department of the Interior continued to exercise its authorities relating to the supervision of Indian Gaming as provided in IGRA.

In early 1993, Chairman Hope explained that the Commission had 17 employees and that an estimated 175 Tribes operated 200 gaming operations. By October 1993, the Commission had a staff of 27, which included three Commissioners, the General Counsel, six field representatives, financial analysts and administrative support staff.

Since 1993, the Commission has grown, as the industry has grown. We have gone from 27 employees in 1993 to 73 in 2000 to 126 in 2010. Currently, the agency has seven regional offices located in Phoenix, Portland, Sacramento, St. Paul, Washington, D.C., Tulsa and Oklahoma City, along with three satellite offices in Temeculah, California, Rapid City, South Dakota and Flowood, Mississippi. Since becoming operational, the Commission has continued to review, amend and promulgate regulations as the gaming industry has matured. The Commission is currently in the process of reviewing its regulations and seeking input from the Tribes and the public in an effort to identify areas of improvement and any needed changes.

The Commission is the Federal civil regulatory agency for Indian gaming. As the Committee is well aware, several Congresses have considered legislation that would authorize Internet poker or Internet gaming. None of the Internet gaming bills currently pending before Congress provides NIGC with a regulatory role. Thus, NIGC is not in a position today to speculate on the particulars of any legislative proposal for which there is no clear role contemplated for NIGC.

This concludes my testimony. Thank you again, Chairman Akaka, Vice Chairman Barrasso, Senator Franken and members of the Committee for your time and attention today. I am happy to answer any questions that you may have for me.

[The prepared statement of Mr. Roberts follows:]

PREPARED STATEMENT OF LAWRENCE S. ROBERTS, GENERAL COUNSEL, NATIONAL INDIAN GAMING COMMISSION

Chairman Akaka, Vice-Chairman Barrasso, and Members of the Committee. I want to begin by thanking you for inviting the Commission to testify today. My name is Lawrence Roberts and I am a member of the Oneida Nation of Wisconsin. It is an honor to appear before you to testify in my capacity as General Counsel of the National Indian Gaming Commission (NIGC or Commission). Today, I will provide a brief overview of the Commission's history as well as the current size and location of NIGC offices today. This overview will hopefully prove to be helpful as the Committee proceeds with its hearing today.

The Indian Gaming Regulatory Act (IGRA) became law on October 17, 1988 and created the National Indian Gaming Commission (NIGC), a federal civil regulatory agency. Mr. Anthony Hope, the first Chairman of the NIGC, started at the Commission on May 25, 1990, more than a year-and-a-half after the enactment of IGRA. The second Commissioner, Mr. Joel Frank, Sr. was sworn into office on November 26, 1990 and the third commissioner, Ms. Jana McKeag, joined the Commission almost a year after the Chairman on April 10, 1991. In these early days, NIGC overcame common hurdles of a new agency before becoming operational, such as securing office space, hiring staff and promulgating initial regulations.

The agency proposed its first regulations on May 29, 1991, approximately a year into Chairman Hope's tenure. The first set of regulations concerned the collection of fees. Since the NIGC is now funded entirely on fees assessed on tribal gaming operations, promulgation of these regulations was a top priority and critical to the Commission. The

Fee regulations were finalized on August 15, 1991, nearly three years after the enactment of IGRA.

The Fee regulations were followed by regulations addressing other statutory duties of the Commission such as approval of gaming ordinances, approval of management contracts, and compliance and enforcement procedures. These and other regulations became effective on February 22, 1993. Thus, it was not until 1993 that the NIGC began to fully carry out its responsibilities under IGRA. The delay in promulgating regulations governing the approval of ordinances and management contracts may have slowed the entry of tribes into the gaming arena. During this interim period, the Department of the Interior continued to exercise authorities relating to the supervision of Indian gaming as provided in IGRA.

In early 1993, Chairman Hope explained that the Commission had seventeen employees and that an estimated 175 tribes operated 200 gaming operations. By October 1993, the NIGC had a staff of twenty-seven which included the three Commissioners, the General Counsel, six field representatives, financial analysts and administrative support staff.

Since 1993, the Commission has grown as the industry has grown. We have gone from twenty-seven employees in 1993 to seventy-three employees in 2000 to one hundred and twenty-six in 2010. Currently the agency has seven regional offices, along with three satellite offices located throughout the nation. Since becoming operational, the Commission has continued to review, amend and promulgate regulations as the Indian gaming industry has matured. The Commission is currently in the process of reviewing its regulations and seeking input from Tribes and the public in an effort to identify areas

of improvement and any needed changes

The Commission is the Federal civil regulatory agency for Indian gaming, with

the Department of the Interior performing discrete functions pursuant to IGRA. As the

Committee is well aware, several Congresses have considered legislation that would

authorize internet poker or internet gaming. None of the internet gaming bills currently

pending before Congress provide NIGC with a regulatory role. NIGC is not in a position

to speculate on the particulars of any legislative proposal for which there is no clear role

contemplated for NIGC.

This concludes my testimony. Thank you again, Chairman Akaka, Vice-

Chairman Barrasso and Members of the Committee for your time and attention today. I

am happy to answer any questions that you may have for me.

The CHAIRMAN. Thank you. Thank you very much, Mr. Roberts.

The NIGC is funded out of a percentage of Tribal gaming revenues. How long was the NIGC funded out of Federal budget appropriations before the Tribal gaming revenues were sufficient to fund the agency's operations?

Mr. ROBERTS. Thank you for your question, Mr. Chairman—1998 was the first year in which the Commission did not receive appropriations from Congress. Prior to 1998, Tribal fees were capped at $1.5 million annually, and the remainder of our funding, of the agency, came from appropriations.

The CHAIRMAN. It has been reported, Mr. Roberts, that the Nevada Gaming Control Board will begin accepting applications for Internet poker licenses in February. If Tribes were to begin submitting ordinances to the NIGC for Internet poker, what would the NIGC's response be, do you think?

Mr. ROBERTS. Thank you for your question, Mr. Chairman. I can't speculate as to how the Chairwoman would approach such an ordinance. I can tell you that generally speaking, we review gaming ordinances on a case-by-case basis and review them for consistency with IGRA. And so in an ordinance that would raise a unique situation like the one you are raising, we may, for example, reach out to the Tribe for further legal analysis on that ordinance. And we would probably also reach out and work with some of our sister agencies like the Department of Justice who may be implicated by some of those issues.

The CHAIRMAN. If Congress enacted legislation that made the NIGC the regulator for Tribal Internet gaming, do you think the agency would be prepared to step into that role?

Mr. ROBERTS. Mr. Chairman, thank you again for your question. I would say that NIGC is as capable as any other Federal agency. NIGC, as I mentioned in my oral testimony, is the only agency solely dedicated to the regulation of Indian gaming. But at this time, NIGC has not been identified in any current legislation and so without knowing what our role would be, I can't really comment on NIGC's regulation of Internet gaming.

The CHAIRMAN. Thank you very much for your responses.

Senator Franken, do you have any questions?

Senator FRANKEN. Yes, I do, Mr. Chairman.

In fact, I will continue along in the same vein. I know that in your capacity you have seen the benefits that gaming, the gaming industry has to Indian Country. It is unquestionable. And anybody who has been to Indian Country can see it, especially for those bands and Tribes that are located geographically in an optimum place to take advantage of it. And many of them are generous with other Tribes as well. And this again, in my own experience, I have seen schools and water treatment and economic development, all this come from gaming.

And I would imagine that there is some feeling at the NIGC and I know you are Chief Counsel there, right?

Mr. ROBERTS. Yes, sir.

Senator FRANKEN. So maybe this isn't your job, but you are here as witness. What is the feeling about Internet gambling? I would imagine it is something that threatens Indian gaming. I imagine it would be something that Indians would be very wary of and would want some stake in, if it were to become part of the gaming horizon.

Mr. ROBERTS. Thank you, Senator Franken, for your question. The Commission has heard from some Tribes that are in favor of Internet gaming and some Tribes that are not. As the regulator, the Federal agency that regulates Indian gaming, we don't take a position on whether that is going to be beneficial to the industry. We are focused more on the regulation.

Senator FRANKEN. Okay. If Internet gaming were made legal tomorrow, fully legal, and your Commission would have a role in regulating Tribal Internet gaming or Internet gaming that is related to Tribes, do you think that IGRA would have to be rewritten in any way in order for the Commission to take on that role?

Mr. ROBERTS. Thank you for your question, Senator. I understand your concern. It is a hard question to answer in the abstract, because I don't know. There is no bill out there that provides roles and responsibilities for us.

Senator FRANKEN. Right. I understand.

Mr. ROBERTS. So it is hard to lay out whether that would actually need to be part of an amendment of IGRA or not in the abstract. I think it really depends on how Congress defines our role.

Senator FRANKEN. I see. But Congress would have to create a definition. I mean, if Congress were to say, okay, the Indian side of this is going to be regulated by IGRA, we definitely have to put that legislation in and say, it would have to be in the legislation, obviously, right?

Mr. ROBERTS. Yes, and if Congress, as with any legislation, we would implement our statutory duties as Congress directs us to.

Senator FRANKEN. Thank you. Thank you, Mr. Chairman.

The CHAIRMAN. Thank you very much, Senator Franken.

Now I would like to call on our Vice Chairman, Senator Barrasso, for any remarks and questions he may have.

STATEMENT OF HON. JOHN BARRASSO,
U.S. SENATOR FROM WYOMING

Senator BARRASSO. Mr. Chairman, thank you for your continued leadership. I would like to follow up on one of the questions that you asked—I think it is along the same lines of the question Senator Franken has just asked. Because the Indian Gaming Regulatory Act established the National Indian Gaming Commission as the Federal regulatory agency for Tribal gaming, there have been some suggestions that the Commission should also play a role as regulator for Internet Tribal gaming. And I think Senator Franken asked if we would actually have to rewrite the law.

Along those lines, if the Commission is the regulator, how will the agency either have to be changed or strengthened to accommodate this expansion of Tribal gaming, and maybe the impacts on your budget, and things we should be looking at.

Mr. ROBERTS. Thank you, Vice Chairman Barrasso, for your question. I think that in terms of how the agency addresses a new role, if you decide to provide that role to the Commission, what we would do is we would look at that legislation, evaluate what our responsibilities are and move forward at this time. In terms of what additional funding, for example, would the Commission need to regulate Internet gaming, that is in large part dependent on the roles Congress sets forth for us.

So it is hard to, because we are not named in any legislation, it is hard to speculate as to what we would need.

Senator BARRASSO. Thank you, Mr. Chairman. We should move on, and thank you.

The CHAIRMAN. Thank you very much, Senator.

I would now like to call on Senator Tom Udall for any opening remarks and questions that you may have.

STATEMENT OF HON. TOM UDALL,
U.S. SENATOR FROM NEW MEXICO

Senator UDALL. Thank you, Senator Akaka, very much. And thank you for holding this hearing. I know that this is a very important subject, the future of Internet gaming, and what is at stake for the Tribes. I know that the Tribes do have a lot at stake in this, so this is no doubt something that we need to hear about from all the various panels that we have here.

This question may have been asked, but I wanted to ask you a couple of questions here. Do you believe that the ongoing Internet poker that is conducted through international sites has already been a deterrent or a benefit to gaming Tribes? How do you ensure that IGRA is protected in creating a space for Tribal Internet gaming?

Mr. ROBERTS. Thank you, Senator, for your question. In terms of how Internet gaming may impact Tribal revenues, we are focused on the regulatory responsibilities that we have under IGRA. I think some of the later panelists may be able to look at that, but we don't evaluate how competition is impacting Indian gaming.

Senator UDALL. How can we ensure that the needs of all the Tribes are being considered and are included in any potential conversation, such as those that have limited access to technology and those with limited gaming facilities on their lands?

Mr. ROBERTS. It is a difficult issue, because as the question identifies, it is not a one size fits all approach. I think again, Senator, we are focused on performing our regulatory capabilities under IGRA. We haven't been named in any legislation involving Internet poker or Internet gaming. While we are aware of the legislation, we haven't evaluated the legislation to look at the questions that you are asking today. If we were asked to do so, I am sure we would. And we would try to be helpful to this Committee as it considers those questions.

Senator UDALL. What is the general position now with regard to the National Indian Gaming Commission on Internet gaming? You don't have a position? You feel you haven't been asked it?

Mr. ROBERTS. Our general position, Senator, is that we have heard, through our working with Tribes, we have heard some Tribes who are in favor of Internet gaming, some Tribes are not in favor of it. As a regulator of Indian gaming itself, we don't take a position one way or another.

Senator UDALL. And you wouldn't expect to take a position at all in the future?

Mr. ROBERTS. Not that I know of today.

Senator UDALL. What is the position as far as, is there, do you believe, adequate regulation at this point that is under your purview?

Mr. ROBERTS. For Indian gaming under IGRA?

Senator UDALL. Yes.

Mr. ROBERTS. I believe there is adequate regulation.

Senator UDALL. Could you describe a little bit for the Committee the kinds of resources that you have committed to this and what you are doing?

Mr. ROBERTS. Absolutely. We have seven regional offices with a staff of approximately 120 people that work with Tribal gaming regulators on a day-to-day basis and their State counterparts. So on a day-to-day basis of implementing our responsibilities, we are working with, I believe the Chairwoman testified at the July hearing, with approximately 6,000 other actual regulators of Indian gaming. And we feel that we are fully performing our responsibilities under IGRA.

Senator UDALL. Thank you very much. I appreciate it, Chairman Akaka.

The CHAIRMAN. Thank you very much, Senator Udall.

I want to thank you very much, Mr. Roberts, for being here and representing the Commission. I would like to send my best wishes to Tracie Stevens, Chairman of the Commission, and look forward to working together on these issues and maybe even legislation.

Mr. ROBERTS. Thank you.

The CHAIRMAN. And I want to wish you well.

Mr. ROBERTS. Thank you, Mr. Chairman.

The CHAIRMAN. Thank you very much.

We would like to invite the second panel to the witness table. Bruce Bozsum, Chairman of the Mohegan Tribe, and Honorable Glen Gobin, Vice Chairman of the Tulalip Tribes, I want to welcome both of you to this Committee hearing and thank you for being here.

Mr. Bozsum, will you please proceed with your testimony?

STATEMENT OF HON. BRUCE "TWO DOGS" BOZSUM, CHAIRMAN, MOHEGAN TRIBE

Mr. BOZSUM. Thank you, aloha, Chairman Akaka.

The CHAIRMAN. Aloha.

Mr. BOZSUM. Good afternoon, everybody, good afternoon, Vice Chairman Barrasso and members of the Committee. My name is Bruce "Two Dogs" Bozsum. I am the Chairman of the Mohegan Tribe and I am also a ceremonial pipe carrier for my Tribe.

It is a great honor to be here with you today to present testimony on a subject of critical importance to the Mohegan Tribe: Internet gaming, its regulation and what is at stake for Indian Tribes. Nearly four centuries ago, one of our greatest leaders, Sachem Uncas, was confronted by the challenges of protecting our Tribe's sovereignty, traditions and people in the face of European colonization, disease and new technologies previously unknown to our people. Sachem Uncas chose the path of cooperation rather than conflict, and today we continue to follow this path of cooperation.

The technology of Internet gaming presents both an opportunity and a challenge not unlike what Sachem Uncas once faced. Cooperation, not conflict, remains the Mohegan Way. And Chairman Akaka, by actively seeing the input of Tribes today, you are walking in that same path, and we thank you for that.

Indian gaming has been the single biggest economic development success story in Tribal history. Tribes use Indian gaming revenue to fund urgent priorities such as housing and health care for our members, services for our elders and education for our youth. The Mohegan Tribes believes that if done properly, Internet gaming can result in another success story for Tribes. I have set out in my written testimony in greater detail some specific suggestions on how Internet gaming legislation should be shaped.

First, let me note that not all Tribes nationwide agree on all issues surrounding Internet gaming. However, we do agree on some basic principles. Any new law must protect Tribal sovereignty and existing Tribal government rights. As set out in the resolution, as you have seen from NIGA, and that is who you will also hear from today, Mohegan endorses these principles wholeheartedly.

Our bottom line is this: any Federal legislation authorizing Internet gaming must protect and preserve the gains Tribal nations have made under IGRA. And at the same time, it must allow us the opportunity to compete on a fair and level playing field with all other interests in any legalized Internet gaming markets. Given a fair chance, Indian Tribes can compete and be as successful as anyone else.

And all Tribes would agree that there must not be a head start for Nevada, New Jersey, or anyone else into the Internet gaming market. We ask you to reject any provisions which use concocted formulas or restrictions under various guises of consumer protection and experienced operator requirements to delay or excludes Tribes entirely from competing in the Internet gaming market. For competition to be fair, it must be open to everyone at the same time and on a level playing field.

I will conclude by summarizing some specific process and policy considerations that we ask you and your colleagues to take into account. First, the time-honored policy of Tribal consultation should be followed, and Tribes should be included in every step of the legislative process and regulation development on Internet gaming.

Second, the Internet gaming legalization should be initially developed and advanced only through the regular committee order with input from Tribal stakeholders. It is imperative that Internet gaming language not be developed behind closed doors. We urge you to insist that this Committee on Indian Affairs be fully involved at each step, because it has direct responsibility for and expertise on Tribal sovereignty and Federal Indian law.

Third, each of the Internet gaming proposals should be improved to ensure that Tribal government and Tribal gaming facilities are authorized to operate Internet gaming sites on a level playing field. Here are our suggestions to enhance the legislative proposals.

Expressly authorize Indian Tribes to accept legal wagers from players not physically located on Tribal lands. Otherwise, an unintended consequence of some IGRA provisions would put Tribes in a competitive disadvantage.

Protect existing Tribal-State gaming compacts and clarify that Tribal Internet gaming will operate outside the IGRA compact and system so as to level the playing field with non-Tribal competitors.

Respect the differences between revenue sharing agreements and taxation. Any legislation must honor the principle that governments don't tax governments.

Utilize existing Tribal gaming regulatory structures. Tribes are experts at regulating all forms of legalized gaming and regulate far more gaming activity than Nevada or New Jersey.

Strictly enforce against unlicensed and unregulated sites. If these sites are not shut down right away, the regulated market will fail and the investments made at creating honest, legal operations will be lost.

Introduce poker only in phase one. It is Mohegan's belief that a poker-only introduction would allow the U.S. market to establish an appropriate regulatory scheme.

Encourage the formation of Tribal Internet gaming coalitions by cooperation on a nationwide basis. We believe that Tribes will be able to succeed at Internet gaming with all potential competitors, including Nevada, as long as there is a level playing field.

In conclusion, the Mohegan Tribe is very grateful to you, Chairman Akaka, and to this Committee, for seeking Tribal input on Internet gaming, on the legislation. We look forward to working with you closely in the coming weeks and months and hope that together, in full Tribal consultation, we can achieve the goal of safe, secure, regulated and fair Internet gaming. Thank you.

[The prepared statement of Mr. Bozsum follows:]

PREPARED STATEMENT OF HON. BRUCE "TWO DOGS" BOZSUM, CHAIRMAN, MOHEGAN TRIBE

Good afternoon Chairman Akaka, Vice Chairman Barrasso, and Members of the Committee. My name is Bruce "Two Dogs" Bozsum, and I am the Chairman of the Mohegan Tribe and also a Pipe Carrier. It is a great honor to be with you here today to present testimony on the important subject of Internet Gaming, its regulation, and what's at stake for Indian tribes.

Mr. Chairman, the Mohegan Tribe has a long and proud history going back many thousands of years. During the 1600s, one of our greatest leaders, Sachem Uncas, was confronted by the challenges of protecting our Tribe's sovereignty, traditions, and people in the face of European colonization, disease, and new technologies previously unknown to our people. The decision he made in how to deal with these challenges was of vital importance to our future.

Sachem Uncas chose the path of cooperation, rather than conflict. This path served him and our people well, and started a tradition known as "The Mohegan Way". This tradition has been passed down through the generations by our ancestors to the present day, where our people continue to live and work cooperatively both within the Tribe and the non-Indian community.

The technology of Internet gaming presents both an opportunity and a challenge to tribes engaged in gaming—similar in some ways to the rapid changes Sachem Uncas once faced in his world long ago. Chairman Akaka, we at the Mohegan Tribe are grateful that since the day you were elected, you have shown your great respect for tribal sovereignty by actively seeking the input of tribes in all legislation to ensure that we are treated fairly. In doing so, you have shown your desire for cooperation, rather than conflict, and we sincerely thank you for this stance.

As you know, Indian gaming has been the single biggest economic development success story in tribal history. Since the enactment of the Indian Gaming Regulatory Act of 1988, tribes have opened 419 gaming facilities across 28 states, creating over half a million new jobs. These tribal casinos are currently generating nearly $27 billion in much-needed revenue, which is used to fund urgent tribal priorities such as housing and health care for our members, services for our elders, and education for our youth. I would also add that tribes nationwide also share a significant portion of the revenue we earn from gaming with state and local governments, helping our neighbors meet the needs of their citizens as well.

I am proud that the Mohegan Tribe has been part of the success story of Indian gaming. Our tribal government runs one of the largest and most successful tribal casinos in the United States. Our extensive experience in regulating gaming activities, protecting consumers, and exercising our sovereign rights as a tribal nation gives us unique insights into the impacts that Internet Gaming may have on Land-Based tribal gaming.

The Mohegan Tribe believes that, if done properly, Internet Gaming can result in another success story for tribes. The balance of my testimony today will discuss the ways in which we feel legislation would best be crafted to allow tribes the opportunity to be successful in Internet Gaming.

As you may know, not all tribes nationwide agree on all the issues surrounding Internet Gaming. Many are still forming their opinions on the topic. However, there are some areas of bedrock principle, such as protecting tribal sovereignty and existing tribal government rights, which virtually all tribes agree on. The National Indian Gaming Association has put forth a resolution stating these principles, which I understand has already been presented to you.

In addition to these principles, I would venture to say that there is at least one other area in which there would be universal agreement among tribes: Any federal legislation authorizing Internet Gaming must ensure that Indian Country can protect and preserve the gains tribal nations have made under IGRA, while at the same time allowing us the opportunity to compete on a fair and level playing field with other gaming interests in any legalized Internet Gaming market.

I cannot stress this point too strongly. Policy changes in recent years have allowed tribes to prove that, when given a fair chance, they can compete and be as successful as anyone else. For far too long in our nation's history, tribes had the deck stacked against them through unfair treatment which has greatly hurt our peoples. Now is not the time to return to those misguided policies of the bad old days. That is why all tribes would agree that there cannot and must not be a head start for Nevada, New Jersey, or other commercial casino states into the Internet Gaming market. Any legislation which uses concocted formulas or restrictions under various guises of "consumer protection" and "experienced operator requirements" to delay or exclude tribes entirely from competing in the Internet gaming market must be categorically rejected. For competition to be fair, it must be played on a level field.

So, how should legislation be crafted in order to create this level playing field, which gives tribes a chance to compete fairly, protects tribal sovereignty, and preserves the gains of IGRA? The Mohegan Tribe believes that there are both process and policy considerations which would be of great help in achieving this goal.

First, two key process considerations. The time-honored policy of tribal consultation should be honored, and tribes should be included in every step of the legislative process on Internet Gaming from drafting the bills through regulatory rulemaking after a law has been enacted. Mr. Chairman, there is no doubt that you understand the consultation process well, as demonstrated by the fact that you are holding this hearing today. As you know, every single piece of successful legislation dealing with Indian Country over the past few decades, many of which you have been personally involved with, has its roots in consultation with tribes BEFORE the initial bills were even drafted or introduced. Federal Internet Gaming legislation should not be an exception to this policy of tribal consultation. There is little doubt that if it is enacted, Internet Gaming legislation will have the most significant impact on tribal gaming since the passage of IGRA. Therefore, tribes must be consulted throughout the entire process of legislation and implementation of regulations, and their input given serious consideration.

A second key consideration is the legislative process itself. It is in the best interest of all concerned, particularly tribes, that Internet Gaming legalization should be initially developed and advanced through regular committee order. We realize that as a practical matter, it is likely that such a bill might have to be attached to another, larger piece of legislation to achieve final passage. However, it is imperative that whatever language ultimately does pass is not developed behind closed doors and with little or no input from tribal stakeholders. The specific legislative language should be fully vetted first by the committees of jurisdiction, particularly by those such as this Senate Committee on Indian Affairs with direct responsibility for and expertise on tribal issues and Federal Indian law, to ensure that Internet Gaming legislation is constructed in a fair way which respects tribal sovereignty and existing law.

Now, I will address the key policy considerations. The Mohegan Tribe has conducted an extensive analysis of the numerous bill drafts and proposals circulated on Internet Gaming in the last several years. In general, we believe that much of this legislation is on the right path. However, it is our strong belief that each of these proposals can and should be further modified and enhanced from its current form. From our perspective, these modifications and enhancements must advance our most critical priority, that of ensuring that Tribal Governments and Tribal Gaming Facilities are authorized to operate Internet Gaming sites ON A LEVEL PLAYING FIELD.

The following are our suggestions for additional improvements:

- A guarantee that Indian tribes may accept otherwise legal wagers from players not physically located on tribal lands when the wager is placed. Under IGRA, tribal government gaming operations are only allowed to accept wagers which are placed by individuals who are physically located on tribal lands at the time the wager is placed. In the area of Internet Gaming, this is problematic as many tribes will choose to operate their Internet Gaming sites on the reservation, but will need to be afforded the same rights as non-tribal competitors to accept wagers from customers located in areas that have not opted out of the federal regulatory framework. In order to do so, legislation must include a clear and unequivocal provision that tribes will not be subject to the geographic limitations of the Indian Gaming Regulatory Act to the extent they are conducting Internet Gaming under federal licenses. Failure to include such a provision would be inherently unfair to tribal governments and burden them with an extreme competitive disadvantage. Furthermore, allowing tribal governments to offer Internet wagering from our tribal lands to prospective customers anywhere would allow tribes, and our customers, to further benefit from the internal controls, safeguards, and experienced regulatory systems that tribes have developed to regulate gaming under IGRA and state gaming compacts. Indeed, the experience of many tribes in regulating gaming, and the testing and certifying of gaming equipment exceeds that of many states and is an asset which federal Internet Gaming legislation should capitalize upon rather than disregard. The position of my Tribe is that this guarantee would be absolutely critical.

- Respect existing Tribal-State Gaming Compacts and clarify that tribal Internet Gaming will operate outside the IGRA compacting system. As you are aware, IGRA requires that tribes and states must enter into a compact if any type of Class III gaming (house-banked games) are to be offered by a tribe. These compacts usually require a tribe to share revenue from Class III activities with a state. Some of the Internet Gaming legislation in circulation would allow a very broad range of Class III games to be offered online by tribal and non-tribal gaming operators, while most tribal-state compacts currently allow only selected Class III games to be offered by tribes. In some states, existing compacts actually preclude tribes from offering any form of Internet gaming whatsoever. A provision must be added to the Internet Gaming legislation that clarifies that all games offered under its auspices are exempt from IGRA compacting, allowing tribes to compete on a level playing field with non-tribal competitors.

- Reflect the differences between revenue sharing agreements and taxation. Just like states, tribal governments are not subject to federal taxation. Like all governments, tribal governments are not subject to taxation by state governments nor can they tax state governments, just as one state can never tax another. Instead, when a tribe agrees to give any payments related to tribal gaming activities to a state, it is done so under a tribal-state revenue sharing agreement that is negotiated between two co-equal sovereigns. This is a system that has been proven to work to the benefit of both tribal and state governments. Any federal Internet Gaming legislation should conform to this standard and contemplate the negotiation of tribal-state revenue sharing agreements on tribal government Internet Gaming activities. Taxation should be properly applied, as it currently is, to commercial gaming enterprises, while where appropriate, tribal activities should be governed by negotiated revenue-sharing agreements.

- Current tribal gaming regulatory structures are working well and should be the foundation of a regulatory system for tribal Internet Gaming. For nearly 25 years, the IGRA model of tribal gaming regulation has worked well. Tribes have developed an extensive range of expertise in regulating all forms of legalized gaming, as well as certifying gaming equipment, vendors, and support systems. Tribal government regulatory agencies currently regulate far more gaming activity in the U.S. than any state, including Nevada or New Jersey. At the federal level, tribal regulators have worked in a strong collaborative relationship with the National Indian Gaming Commission, and with state gaming regulators under the terms of many tribal-state compacts. In contrast, some proposals in Congress would have the Department of the Treasury or the Department of Commerce take the lead role on regulating Internet Gaming. These agencies have no experience whatsoever in gaming regulation, and little experience in interacting with Indian nations. Charging these agencies with new regulatory missions far outside the scope of their experience and expertise is not a good idea. Instead, we should stay with the proven system of regulating tribal gaming activities established by IGRA.

- Some licensing and regulatory provisions can be strengthened further. Access to gaming facilities, careful screening of all persons with access to or responsibility for gaming areas or gaming funds, and testing and certification of all gaming equipment are all key principles to successful gaming regulation. Requiring all Internet Gaming facilities to be located domestically would greatly enhance regulation by ensuring regulator access at all times. Background checks and licensing should be required of all employees, not just a select few. At our tribal government gaming facility, every employee from the CEO down to janitorial help must be licensed, with higher scrutiny for key employees and others in sensitive positions. This protects our facility from being penetrated by unsuitable persons at all levels, ensuring the security of our operations. Finally, testing and certification of software and other equipment used for Internet Gaming will be critical. If anything, the nature of Internet Gaming requires an even higher confidence level by the player that the game being played is honest. Just as we currently test and certify every piece of equipment used for gaming at our brick-and-mortar facilities, so too should all software, hardware, and other systems used for Internet Gaming be subject to intensive testing and certification prior to use to assure players they are wagering on a fair and honest game.

- Strict enforcement against unlicensed sites. One of the reasons that tribal and commercial brick-and-mortar gaming facilities are successful is that any unlawful or unregulated facilities are immediately shut down. We believe that similar measures in Internet Gaming will be even more vital to the success of legalized and regulated sites. If unlicensed and unregulated sites are able to offer their product to American citizens, free of the obligation to follow the rules and obey regulations, these sites will flourish at the expense of those obeying the law. This cannot be allowed to happen, or a regulated system will fail, those who support it will be discredited, and investments made in creating honest, legal operations will be lost.

- Introduce poker-only in Phase I. Perceived competition to state lotteries and brick-and-mortar facilities from Internet slots would create powerful opposition to full Internet Gaming. It is our belief that a poker-only introduction would allow the U.S. market to establish appropriate regulatory schemes and still generate a significant new level of revenue, economic activity, and jobs.
- Encourage the formation of Tribal Internet Gaming Coalitions. It is a well-known fact that when tribes work together to protect tribal interests, they are extremely successful. In the field of Internet Gaming, we believe that the principle of tribes working together would be best expressed in broad-based national coalitions of tribes working together to offer Internet Gaming to customers throughout the country. By working together on a nationwide basis, we believe that tribes will be able to compete successfully with all potential competitors, including Nevada, as long as there is a level playing field. A successful precedent has already been set under IGRA by a number of tribes who have worked together in offering linked and progressive slot machine jackpots to the benefit of all involved. We would urge that any federal legislation on Internet gaming be drafted in such a way as to ensure there are no barriers to Tribal Internet Gaming coalitions, and if possible, should encourage them, so we can duplicate this IGRA success in the Internet Gaming arena.

Once again, the Tribe greatly appreciates your interest in tribal input on this important subject. It is our hope that you will strongly consider the enhancements we have suggested in our testimony to any Internet Gaming legislation which may come before your Committee or the full Senate.

We look forward to working with you closely in the coming weeks and months, and hope to together achieve the goal of safe, secure, regulated Internet Gaming.

The CHAIRMAN. Thank you very much, Chairman Bozsum.

Mr. Vice Chairman Gobin, will you please proceed with your testimony?

STATEMENT OF HON. GLEN GOBIN, VICE CHAIRMAN, TULALIP TRIBES

Mr. GOBIN. Good afternoon, Chairman Akaka, Vice Chairman Barrasso and Committee members. My name is TE CHUHT, Glen Gobin. I am the Vice Chairman of Tulalip Tribes, and I would like to thank you for the opportunity to testify today.

I would also like to thank you for having this hearing and recognizing the potential impacts of Internet gambling in Indian Country. Although I am here today to testify on behalf of Tulalip Tribes, I believe that our views are not unique to Tulalip.

The Tulalip Tribes sees legalization of Internet gambling as a direct threat to the economic growth in Indian Country, and we do not support legislation that legalizes Internet gambling. In 1988, Congress passed the Indian Gaming Regulatory Act, known as IGRA. IGRA provides a statutory basis with the intent to promote Tribal economic development, self-sufficiency and strong Tribal government. IGRA has been by far the most significant piece of legislation since self-determination that has given Indian Tribes the economic opportunity to meet the needs of its membership.

Today, Indian gaming accounts for $26.5 billion annually to this Nation's economy. These dollars do not stay within the reservation boundaries.

Historically, Tribes have not always had the economic means to meet even the basic needs of its membership. Indian dollars today have gone to build infrastructure, such as roads, bridges, underground utilities, provide fire protection, police protection, medical services. These improvements and services are developed at a higher rate in Indian Country than any other jurisdiction in the Nation.

Tulalip is a great example of this. In the year 2000, Tulalip created the Consolidated Borough of Quil Ceda Village, a Tribal municipality unique within the United States. The village was created to enhance and diversify the Tribal economy. Indian gaming revenue supported this infrastructure development, and allowed Tulalip to attract quality nationally known businesses to the reservation.

Today, over $30 million a year in State sales tax is collected from Quil Ceda Village with no State services being provided back to the Tribe. Although we may not agree with the State collection of these sales taxes, what everyone can agree on is the benefit that tax dollars bring to the economy. This type of diversification can be seen across Indian Country and is a direct result of gaming revenues.

Employment in Indian Country has also increased dramatically since the passage of IGRA with Tribal gaming enterprises often being among the largest employers in their respective communities. Tulalip is now the third largest employer in Snohomish County, behind Boeing and the Everett Navy Base. We signed our first gaming compact in 1991. At that time, Tulalip had roughly 350 employees. Today we directly employ over 3,500 people in government operations and Tribal government enterprises. The majority of these employees are non-members with liveable wages and full health benefits.

Coupled with the other business developments that are located within the village, over 6,000 jobs have been created. Again, this is a direct result of Indian gaming. While Tulalip recognizes that not all Tribes have grown in the same manner, the positive changes and successes seen in Indian Country as a result of Indian gaming cannot be understated. IGRA has been able to provide for development where no development was possible, to give opportunities where there were none before, and has allowed for true Tribal self-determination.

There is a lot at stake for Tribes and the local economies where Indian gaming enterprises are located and have been able to thrive. Tulalip feels legalization of Internet gambling comes at a risk to Tribal economies and the tremendous economic growth that has occurred in Indian Country and the surrounding communities. Of the $60 billion gaming dollars that are generated in the U.S. economy from both commercial and Indian gaming, Indian gaming dollars make up over 40 percent. The proponents who seek to legalize Internet gambling say that it will create $41 billion over the next 10 years. However, let us not forget that Indian gaming will provide $265 billion within that same time frame.

Proposed Internet gaming legislation ignores long-established policies and principles regarding Tribal sovereignty. The legislation dismisses the regulatory system established under IGRA that not only protects the customer but the integrity of the games, and ignores the widely-held rule that governments do not tax another government. Moreover, Tribal gaming dollars are already taxed at 100 percent by their own government.

Tulalip does not support legalization of Internet gambling. But if legislation does come forward, we urge a full and open legislative process, allowing Tribes to voice their concerns and provide input.

As I wrap up my testimony, I would like to state that the Tulalip Tribes fully supports the six principles regarding legalization of Internet gambling put forward by both the National Indian Gaming Association and the National Congress of American Indians. Again, I thank the Committee for the opportunity to hear some of the concerns from Tulalip and Indian Country.

[The prepared statement of Mr. Gobin follows:]

PREPARED STATEMENT OF HON. GLEN GOBIN, VICE CHAIRMAN, TULALIP TRIBES

Introduction

Good afternoon Chairman Akaka, Ranking Member Barrasso and Committee Members, my name is, TE CHUHT, Glen Gobin, I am the Vice-Chairman of the Tulalip Tribes. I would like to thank you for this opportunity to testify today on behalf of my Tribal Nation. We would also like to thank you for having this hearing and recognizing the potential impacts of Internet gambling in Indian Country. Although I am here today to testify on behalf of the Tulalip Tribes, I believe that our views are not unique to Tulalip.

The Tulalip Tribes are the successors in interest to the Snohomish, Snoqualmie, and Skykomish Tribes and other Tribes and bands signatory to the Treaty of Point Elliot in 1855. On behalf of the Tulalip Tribes, we see **legalization of Internet gambling as a direct threat to the economic growth in Indian Country and we do not support any proposals that legalize Internet Gambling.**

Background: Positive Impacts of Indian Gaming

In 1988, Congress passed the Indian Gaming Regulatory Act, known as IGRA. IGRA provides a statutory basis with the intent to promote tribal economic development, self-sufficiency, and strong tribal governments (25 U.S.C. 2701). IGRA has been, by far, the most significant piece of legislation since self-determination that has given Indian Tribes the economic opportunity to meet the needs of its membership without constraints that are often associated with outside financial funding.

Today, Indian gaming accounts for $26.5 billion annually to this nation's economy. These dollars do not stay within the reservation boundaries. Historically, Indian Tribes have not always had the economic means to meet even the basic needs of its membership. Indian Gaming dollars today have gone to build infrastructure such as roads, bridges, underground utilities, provide fire protection, police protection, and medical services. These improvements and services are developed at a higher rate in Indian Country than any other jurisdiction in the nation.

The Tulalip Tribal Council created the Consolidated Borough of Quil Ceda Village in the year 2000, a tribal municipality, unique within the United States. Indian gaming revenues supported the infrastructure development within the Village and allowed Tulalip to attract quality nationally known businesses to the reservation. The Village was created to enhance and diversify our tribal economy. Today, over $30 million a year in Washington state sales tax is collected from Quil Ceda Village, with no state services being provided back to the Tribe. Although we may not agree with the state collection of these sale taxes, what everyone can agree on is the benefit that tax dollars bring to the Washington state economy. This type of diversification can be seen across Indian Country, and is a direct result of Indian gaming revenues.

Employment in Indian Country has also increased dramatically since the passage of IGRA. Tribal gaming enterprises are often the largest employers in their respective communities; such is the case for the Tulalip Tribes, which is the third largest employer in Snohomish County behind Boeing and the Everett Navy Base. Tulalip signed its first gaming compact in 1991. At that time Tulalip had roughly 350 employees. Today, we directly employ over 3500 people in government operations and tribal government enterprises, the majority of these employees are non-members with livable wages and full health benefits. Coupled with the other business development that is located within the Village, over 6000 jobs have been created. This is a direct result of Indian gaming.

While Tulalip recognizes that not all Tribes have grown in the same manner, the positive changes and successes seen in Indian Country as a result of Indian gaming cannot be understated. IGRA has been able to provide for development where no development was possible, to give opportunities where there were none before, and has allowed for true tribal self-determination.

Views Opposing Federal Legalization of Internet Gambling

There is a lot at stake for Tribes and the local economies where Indian gaming enterprises are located and have been able to thrive and we strongly oppose any proposals to legalize Internet gambling that threaten these economies.

Of the $60 billion gaming dollars that are generated within the US economy from both Commercial and Indian gaming, Indian gaming dollars make up over 40%. The proponents who seek to legalize Internet gambling say that it will create $41 billion over the next 10 years, however, let us not forget that Indian gaming will provide $265 billion within this same time frame.

The proposals to legalize Internet gambling also ignore long established policies and principles regarding tribal sovereignty. The proposed legislation dismisses the regulatory system established under IGRA that not only protects the customer, but the integrity of the games, and ignores the widely held rule that governments do not tax another government. Moreover, tribal Gaming dollars are already taxed at 100% by their own governments in meeting the intent of IGRA, strengthening Tribal governments.

Conclusion

Proposals to legalize Internet gambling comes at too great of a risk to the economic growth that has occurred in tribal economies and the surrounding communities.

If proposals to legalize Internet gambling do move forward, we urge a full and open legislative process allowing all Indian Tribes to voice their concerns and provide input.

Furthermore, the Tulalip Tribes fully supports the six principles regarding legalization of Internet gambling put forward by the National Indian Gaming Association and the National Congress of American Indians, wherein, any and all proposed Federal legislation must respect Tribal sovereignty by ensuring an Indian Tribes right to operate,

regulate, tax, and license Internet gaming and these rights must not be subordinate to any non-federal authority; legislation must not open up IGRA for amendments; legislation must respect existing Tribal-State Compacts; legislation must ensure positive economic benefits to Indian Country; legislation must ensure that Internet gambling authorized by Indian Tribes is available to customers in any locale where Internet gambling is not criminally prohibited; and legislation must be consistent with long-held federal law and policy, tribal revenues must not be taxed.

Again, on behalf of the Tulalip Tribes, I thank the committee for the opportunity to hear some of the concerns from the Tulalip Tribes and Indian Country on legalization of Internet gambling.

The CHAIRMAN. Thank you very much, Vice Chairman Gobin, for your testimony.

Chairman Bozsum, current legislation would not allow Tribes to be both operators and regulators of Internet gaming. Based on your experience in Indian gaming, do you think Tribes can effectively regulate and operate Internet gaming?

Mr. BOZSUM. Thank you for your question, Senator. I believe we already have proven what we can do with our bricks and mortar.

We have demonstrated that with our governments and how we operate. We have done great so far at that.

In our operation alone, our first gaming commissioner was one of the heads of the FBI and was a head of the DEA, and our current commissioner was the Connecticut Commissioner. We take the integrity of our operation very seriously. Everything that we do is clean and above the board. We feel that Tribes do have the technology, they have the experience to do that, to regulate themselves, to work, again, with the other organizations, Federal Government organizations that are involved with us.

I do believe that, I would support, I should say, that a Federal regulatory scheme should be in place that everybody, Tribal and non-Tribal, all conform to the minimum standard of internal controls.

The CHAIRMAN. And so you also believe that they can operate Internet gaming?

Mr. BOZSUM. Yes, we have proven that we already can. Thank you.

The CHAIRMAN. Mr. Gobin, I know that the Tulalip Tribes are opposed to Internet gaming. And you did mention it, you don't want it to be legalized. How do you think your Tribe and others would like to be included in a dialogue on this issue going forward?

Mr. GOBIN. As the issue continues to come forward, Mr. Chairman, I think that it has been stated already that Tribes need to have a seat at the table. We need to be involved in the process to be hearing the concerns. People need to be there that have full knowledge of Indian Country, Indian gaming, full knowledge of IGRA and its application, and with knowledgeable people sitting there partaking.

The CHAIRMAN. Chairman Bozsum, what is your view on whether Internet gaming legislation should be Federal legislation, rather than decided on a State-by-State basis?

Mr. BOZSUM. Thank you for your question, Senator. As a businessman, I am prepared for either one of those to happen. I think everybody should be. There is a greater opportunity, I think, for everything to be Federal, which will make it fair across the board for all Tribes, for all the businesses. And it is a set of rule that everybody will have to follow.

I think it gets more complicated if we go State to State. There may be different rules, there may be different policies or agreements that happen which may, it probably will complicate things, I believe. And it gives an opportunity for people to have more players from further locations, from other States from around the Country to benefit their business.

So I think, I am prepared for either one, Senator, but I think Federal passage is better for everybody.

The CHAIRMAN. Thank you very much for your responses.

Let me call on the Vice Chairman for any remarks and questions he may have.

Senator BARRASSO. Thank you very much, Mr. Chairman. You covered some of the issues and concerns that I have had. Thank you.

The CHAIRMAN. Thank you. Senator Franken, any questions?

Senator FRANKEN. Yes. We see this chart here, and it is a circular chart, so it could be a pie, right? So we see that there is $61 billion in commercial gaming revenue and 43.4 percent goes to Indian Country. We have talked about the tremendous benefits to Indian Country and to Tribes and to Indian people.

Mr. Gobin, what I think, what I take you are fearing is that if we allow or legalize Internet gaming that there will be another pie, we will see another pie, and it may be bigger, but the slice, the part that is for Indian Country will be smaller. Is that what the fear is?

Mr. GOBIN. We believe that it may have direct impact on the gains that Indian Country has had.

Senator FRANKEN. And not only will it be smaller as a percentage of commercial gaming revenue, but it may be just smaller, because people will stop going to Indian Country for gaming and just stay at home?

Mr. GOBIN. Yes. But as has been stated earlier, the proposed Internet gaming is undecided yet.

Senator FRANKEN. Right.

Mr. GOBIN. So we are unsure of what the dynamics are or how that is going to open, we are not sure if it is poker-only or if it is going to be full gamut of casino style gaming and what those impacts might be. If the market opens up, then there is a delusion of the amount of players, and the developers who develop the games will profit, and how that money gets spread out now across, and how Tribes will be able to compete with that. Tribes still are trying to build infrastructure that allows them access to the outside world. And a lot of Tribes don't have that in place yet. So there is some real question, some Tribes are ready to go, others have a long way to go.

Senator FRANKEN. To either of your knowledge, have there been any studies of this? Have there been any studies of the impact on Indian Country of Internet gambling?

Mr. BOZSUM. Maybe not studies, but there is a fact out there that there is over $5 billion illegally being wagered right now going overseas from this Country, it is revenue that we are losing here. That is a pretty good study.

[Laughter.]

Mr. BOZSUM. I just want to point out one thing. This is commercial gaming. About government gaming, I just want to point that out to the board, we have a lot of government gaming here, not commercial gaming that we are talking about today. Just a quick note, I don't know who did that, but that can be fixed later.

Senator FRANKEN. Where is that?

Mr. BOZSUM. It says commercial gaming revenue.

Senator FRANKEN. Where is the Government gaming? Government gaming would be lottery and stuff like that?

Mr. BOZSUM. Tribes, Tribal government.

Senator FRANKEN. No, I know what commercial is. You are pointing at something.

Mr. BOZSUM. These signs are saying commercial gaming. So to the eye it looks like it is all about commercial gaming, not Tribal government gaming. Just the header, that is all. Just a point of interest.

Senator FRANKEN. I see. What you are saying is that some of that commercial gaming is government gaming, it is like lotteries and stuff? Is that what we are saying?

Mr. BOZSUM. I see Tribal gaming on there more than commercial gaming, from what I am reading.

Senator FRANKEN. Well, commercial would be like, I assume Nevada?

Mr. BOZSUM. Vegas, Nevada, Pennsylvania.

Senator FRANKEN. I assume Nevada is Las Vegas, mainly, and Reno, and New Jersey is Atlantic City. And then I don't know what the other ones are, because I don't know. But I am not sure, does anyone know whether State lotteries and those kinds of things are included in here? They are not?

Mr. BOZSUM. They are not. Okay.

Senator FRANKEN. They are not. Okay. There we go.

Mr. BOZSUM. Sorry. But that is a reasonable question. There are some studies that have been out there on the impact that it will have, and the revenue that——

Senator FRANKEN. And do you feel there will be some Tribes that will be winners in this and some Tribes that will be losers in this? In other words, Mr. Gobin, you are basically saying that there are some Tribes that are positioned to take advantage of Internet gaming better than other Tribes, just as there are some Tribes that are better able to take advantage of casino gambling by virtue of their location. Is that something we should look at and study as we go forward?

Mr. GOBIN. Yes.

Mr. BOZSUM. Can I comment on that?

Senator FRANKEN. Yes.

Mr. BOZSUM. The location, the Internet, it is the world wide web, there are no boundaries. So I don't think anybody is going to be limited to what they can do. If it is Federal, it is open for you to go around the Country. So I don't think anybody is at a disadvantage. I think it is an opportunity that Tribes should not miss. If commercial businesses do it, we will never catch up after the fact. And that is why we need a fair and level playing field, and we need to start at the same time as everybody else when it does happen.

Senator FRANKEN. Mr. Chairman, my time is up. I was wondering if Mr. Gobin would like to comment on Mr. Bozsum's remarks, which would be a little at odds with his.

Mr. GOBIN. It is somewhat. Tribes need to be at the table if legislation comes forward, and we need to be able to participate and have access. How that comes forward is the question, and the timing on when that comes forward is the question, to give Tribes ample opportunity to prepare. To think that Tribes are going to compete with someone like Harrah's on the Internet, and my Tribe, Tulalip Tribes, there is no name recognition. So my customer base is severely diminished. Tribes need to have the opportunity to develop, put those systems in place, and if it is turned on tomorrow, I don't believe all Tribes are ready. There may be a handful, but I don't believe the majority of Tribes are ready to go.

Senator FRANKEN. Thank you, Mr. Chairman. Thank you both.

The CHAIRMAN. Thank you very much, Senator Franken.

Senator Udall?

Senator UDALL. Thank you, Mr. Chairman. It is clear from the testimony that Tribal nations will definitely be affected by Internet gaming. The question remains, what will this impact look like. A lot of you call for Tribal consultation. I think both of you have said that in a way in your testimony. Call for Tribal consultation in the development of Internet gaming regulations.

What would this consultation look like to individual Tribes? And does consultation go far enough?

Mr. BOZSUM. I will start. Well, the consultation is always important. Because if you are not at the table, for dinner, you will be dinner at some point. So we need to be there to make sure that there are laws, there are structures put in place that protect Tribes. We do fall under the laws of IGRA, so there are some differences to commercial and Tribal gaming, which we need to work out. I understand that. There are some issues out there. Those are little things that we need to discuss as we go forward.

I think there is an opportunity for Tribal gaming, just as there is for any other person in this Country that wants to go into the business. And we need, again, just to reiterate, we need to make sure that we are at the table working out all the details behind what the policy will be.

Senator UDALL. And I assume part of that will be what Mr. Gobin was saying, that a larger entity like Harrah's or somebody could gear up much quicker than a Tribe, you want a level playing field in that area.

Mr. BOZSUM. That may look like that unless you look at the board over there. The Indian Country line seems a lot higher. I think if we can all get together, and form the coalition I talked about earlier, I think the Tribes may have a little more power than any Harrah's.

Senator UDALL. But as far as their, you don't think there is any difference then as far as the sophistication or the size or anything like that in terms of being able to put it up quickly and put Tribes at a disadvantage?

Mr. BOZSUM. I don't think so. I don't think all commercial businesses are ready to pull the trigger yet, I don't think all Tribes are. But I think a lot of people have been looking at it, and preparing. So it is going to be an equal start, I think, an equal chance for everybody to start at the same time, if it is fair across the board.

Senator UDALL. Thank you. Mr. Gobin?

Mr. GOBIN. And I believe the system that was being presented to pull Tribal leaders nationally across the Country to start to have input on how we are impacted, or how we see benefits of going forward, the problem is, the legislation is undefined. We don't know what the rules or the parameters of the legislation are going to be. So when we are talking about all the benefits, we are talking about from our best case scenario if everything happens in a certain manner. As it stands right now, there are about 250, I believe, gaming operations making this $26.5 billion. The other 400, 250 Tribes, I believe it is, do gaming.

Unless those all connect together, then yes, maybe they can all have the same pool of customers. But if they do it singly, their customer base is not going to be the same as a larger name brand casino operation. So that is where the fear comes in. And again, we don't know if it is poker-only. Current legislation proposal is for poker-only. The revenue projections for poker-only are significantly less than what is being presented by the proponents.

Senator UDALL. And I assume what you would like to see, if this is legislated, is a full, open legislative process where you see the bill, you have an opportunity to comment, there are hearings on it, there is an open markup process and the ability to amend on the Floor of the Senate and all those kinds of things in both the Senate and the House?

Mr. BOZSUM. Yes.

Mr. GOBIN. Yes. But we might ask that there be not any midnight riders attached.

Senator UDALL. Yes, well, that is part of being open and trying to not do things at that hour of the day.

Thank you very much, Mr. Chairman.

The CHAIRMAN. Thank you very much, Senator Udall. Are there further questions?

I would like to thank you very much for your responses, and look forward to continuing to work with you on these issues. So thank you very much for being here.

I would like to invite the third panel to the witness table. Mr. Ernie Stevens, aloha. Chairman of the National Indian Gaming Association. Mr. Stevens is accompanied by Mr. Mark Van Norman, Senior Advisor of the National Indian Gaming Association. Mr. Alfonse D'Amato, Chairman of the Poker Players Alliance. Senator D'Amato is accompanied by Mr. John Pappas, Executive Director of Poker Players Alliance.

Ms. Penny Coleman, Principal of Coleman Indian Law, and Mr. Grant Eve, Manager of Joseph Eve, Certified Public Accounts.

Again, I want to welcome all of you here to the Committee. Mr. Stevens, will you please proceed with your testimony?

STATEMENT OF ERNEST STEVENS, JR., CHAIRMAN, NATIONAL INDIAN GAMING ASSOCIATION; ACCOMPANIED BY MARK VAN NORMAN, SENIOR ADVISOR, NATIONAL INDIAN GAMING ASSOCIATION

Mr. STEVENS. Good afternoon, Mr. Chairman, members of the Committee. Just a quick note, Mr. Chairman, yesterday I spent preparing with my staff for this testimony. It was my 29th anniversary. So I sent two dozen roses instead of the normal one dozen roses. My wife is a great lady, a mother of five and ten grandchildren. She supports the work we do in Washington as long as I don't try to move her here.

The CHAIRMAN. My congratulations to you.

Mr. STEVENS. Thank you, sir.

Good afternoon, Chairman Akaka, Vice Chairman Barrasso and the members of the Committee. Thank you for this opportunity to provide the views of the National Indian Gaming Association on the important issue of Internet gaming. I have to say, it is an honor to again be seated on the panel with Mr. D'Amato. I testified with him just about a month ago. It is again a great honor.

I appreciate the Senators' attempts to understand Indian Country, and I hope we will continue to appreciate why Tribal governments cannot compromise Indian sovereignty. As the Committee knows, more than 200 Indian Tribes use gaming as a means to generate essential Tribal government revenue. Under the Indian Gaming Regulatory Act, that revenue is used to address the severe unmet needs of Tribal communities. Because Indian gaming revenues are used for government purposes, Tribal government revenues are not subject to taxation.

For more than two decades under the Indian Gaming Regulatory Act, Tribes have consistently proven their ability to operate and independently regulate Indian gaming. The success of Indian gaming has been felt across America, creating more than 600,000 American jobs for Indians and non-Indians alike.

Knowing how many people depend on Indian gaming, the legalization of Internet gaming raises significant concerns, Mr. Chairman. In 2010, Tribal leaders conducted more than a dozen meetings to discuss the bills to legalize Internet gaming. This year at our board meeting, in conjunction with our annual trade show, the National Indian Gaming Association established the Internet Gaming Subcommittee and has met several times since its establishment.

Again, this subcommittee is made up entirely of Tribal leaders from throughout Indian Country and their respective support teams. We want to try to understand this industry as well as understanding opportunities for economic development. I think that we have said it time and time again, Mr. Chairman, there is so much unmet need in Indian Country but yet at the same time there are a lot of opportunities here that Indian Country does not want to miss out on. We want to work hard for the benefit of our communities. We have big communities, we have small communities. We have some that are just getting on their feet and we have some, too many, that continue to struggle.

As a result, Tribal leaders nationwide remain unified behind a set of core principles that I would like to now share with you. These committees continue to work hard. I guess that is what I am trying to maybe over-emphasize. But we have worked hard on this issue. And Indian Country is united. We have had resolutions supporting our standpoint. We just met extensively at the National Congress of American Indians in Portland, Oregon.

I just want to share these with you briefly. First, legislation should acknowledge that all Tribes are eligible to operate and regulate Internet gaming. Under the Indian Gaming Regulatory Act, Tribes have proven our ability to both regulate and operate gaming facilities. The expertise should be recognized in this new legislation.

In addition, the National Indian Gaming Commission is the only Federal agency with experience in regulating any form of gaming in the United States. They are the only logical entity to regulate Tribal Internet gaming.

Now, I know that with all due respect to Mr. Roberts, and we appreciated their position, but we speak on behalf of the Tribal leaders. This is two years that we have talked with the leadership and they believe that is the appropriate position, the best way to go. In addition to that, Mr. Chairman, we talked with Tribal regulators throughout these two years. I have asked them to analyze, asked them to prepare, asked them to be ready to deal with this kind of legislation as it comes forward, not for the purposes of promotion, but to understand it and appreciate it.

Second, legislation should allow customers to access Tribal Internet sites as long as it is legal where the customer is located. Again, we have the experience here. Tribes have conducted gaming beyond local Tribal borders for years by linking machines to broadened participation. Internet gaming is the next logical step.

Third, as I stated above, Indian gaming revenue are dedicated to meeting the Tribal community needs. That is essentially, Vice Chairman Gobin said it as well, essentially it is a 100 percent Tribal tax. Legislation should acknowledge that the Tribal Internet revenues must not be taxed by Federal and State.

Fourth, legislation must fully protect Tribal rights under the Indian Gaming Regulatory Act and existing Tribal-State gaming compacts. Tribal-State gaming compacts have been carefully negotiated. Tribes have invested significant resources based on these agreements and they must be honored.

Finally, our principles ask that Congress not amend IGRA as it establishes a new law on Internet gaming. Many Federal laws recognize Indian Tribes as governments outside of Title 25, and Tribes ask Congress to follow that precedent.

These are core principles that Tribal leaders nationwide have united behind. Unfortunately, current Internet gaming proposals, including the bill offered by Congressman Barton, violate these principles and we oppose their passage. My written testimony details our concerns. But a real quick summary as I conclude, Mr. Chairman, the bill fails to treat Tribes as government operators. The bill would tax Tribal government revenue and the bill would violate IGRA and existing Tribal-State compacts.

In closing, Indian gaming has proven to be the most effective tool to help many Tribes address more than a century of failed Federal policies. More than 600,000 American families and more than 200 Tribal communities rely on the current system. If Congress is going to change the system, Tribes ask that the new law follow these principles that will provide fair access to Tribes, that it continue to treat Tribes as governments and it respects the essential government purposes for which Tribal revenue is used.

We appreciate the Committee's oversight and look forward to working with you and your Senate colleagues on this important issue. Thank you for this opportunity. I am prepared to answer any questions when you are done, Mr. Chairman.

[The prepared statement of Mr. Stevens follows:]

PREPARED STATEMENT OF ERNEST STEVENS, JR., CHAIRMAN, NATIONAL INDIAN GAMING ASSOCIATION

Introduction

Good morning Chairman Akaka, Vice Chairman Barrasso, and members of the Committee. My name is Ernie Stevens, Jr., I am a member of the Oneida Nation of Wisconsin and it is my honor to serve as Chairman of the National Indian Gaming Association (NIGA). NIGA is an intertribal association of 184 federally recognized Indian Tribes united behind the mission of protecting and preserving tribal sovereignty and the ability of Tribes to attain economic self-sufficiency through gaming and other economic endeavors. I want to thank you for this opportunity to provide our views on Internet gaming in the United States, and for this Committee's oversight on the issue.

Indian Tribes in the U.S. Federal System of Government

While I know that this Committee is well aware of the conflicted history of the treatment of Indian tribes in the United States, it's necessary to briefly restate some of that history in order to place our views on Internet gaming in proper context.

The U.S. Constitution expressly recognizes Indian tribes as governments. Through treaties with the United States, tribal governments ceded hundreds of millions of acres of their homelands to help build this great Nation. In return, the U.S. promised to preserve remaining tribal lands and tribal sovereignty, and provide for the health, education and general welfare of Indian people. Sadly, many of these treaty promises have been ignored and many more broken.

Generations of failed federal policies ensued, which caused the death of thousands of our ancestors, stole additional millions of acres of tribal land holdings, suppressed our language and culture, and destroyed tribal economies.

Refusing to wait for the federal government to meet its obligations, tribes took matters into their own hands in the 1960s and 1970s when they began using gaming as a means to generate revenue to meet tribal community needs. That's when Presidents Johnson and Nixon adopted the policy of Indian Self-Determination, which promoted the sovereign rights of tribal governments, tribal culture, and tribal economic self-sufficiency. Indian gaming is one of the most successful examples of true Indian Self-Determination.

In 1988, after more than a decade of legal challenges to tribal government gaming by states and commercial gaming interests, Congress stepped in to establish a federal system to regulate and foster Indian gaming through enactment of the Indian Gaming Regulatory Act (IGRA). IGRA acknowledges that Indian tribes, as governments, have the right to both regulate and manage gaming operations. IGRA also mandates that tribal gaming revenues will be used for express tribal government purposes. It also provides that tribal gaming revenues are not subject to taxation. Finally, the Act established a comprehensive regulatory system that involves three levels of government regulation: tribal, federal, and state.

Twenty-three years later, more than 220 Indian tribes have made IGRA work and began to rebuild their once forgotten communities. Indian gaming revenues are working to improve tribal education, health and elder care, rebuild tribal infrastructure and much more. For many tribes, Indian gaming is about jobs. In 2010, Indian gaming created more than 600,000 direct and indirect American jobs. Without question, Indian gaming is putting people to work.

Tribes realize that these gains would not be possible without strong regulation. The Indian gaming regulatory system employs more than 3,400 regulators and state of the art technology to protect tribal revenues. In 2010 alone, tribes spent more than $375 million on regulation. This system is costly, it's comprehensive, and our record and experience shows that it's working.

Indian gaming is not a cure all. However, it has proven to be the best tool for economic development for a great number of Indian tribes. Because of Indian gaming, tribal governments are stronger, our people are healthier, and an entire generation of Indian youth has hope for a better future.

As a result of these gains, all tribes are concerned when Congress considers changing the playing field with regard to gambling. The federal legalization of Internet gaming raises such concerns.

NIGA Views on Federal Legalization of Internet Gambling

Congress has considered various forms of Internet gaming legislation for the past 15 years. The early discussion focused on a prohibition of Internet gaming. This early debate culminated in the enactment of the Unlawful Internet Gambling Enforcement Act (UIGEA). UIGEA was attached as a midnight rider to the Security and Accountability for Every Port Act, P.L. 109–347.[1]

Since enactment of UIGEA, several members of Congress have sought to reverse course and legalize Internet gaming in the United States. Despite our efforts, tribal governments have not been invited to the table during these negotiations or during development of legislation that has been drafted or introduced.

As you have heard today, tribal governments hold various positions on the legalization of Internet gaming. However, despite these disparate views, tribal governments have built a consensus position on Internet gaming. In 2010, tribal leaders met on more than a dozen occasions to discuss the pros and cons of Internet gambling legislation. During these meetings, we heard from experts in the Indian gam-

---

[1] NIGA worked with the Committee's of jurisdiction to ensure that UIGEA protected existing rights under IGRA and in existing tribal-state compacts. As a result, UIGEA exempts intertribal gaming and other forms of gaming authorized under IGRA from the definition of "unlawful Internet gaming."

ing and Internet gaming industry, as well as economists and others. From these meetings, tribal leaders came together to form a unified voice in support of general principles regarding federal legislation that would legalize Internet gaming in the United States.

Our Resolution and accompanying principles acknowledge that Indian country has diverse economies that could be adversely impacted by the federal legalization of Internet gaming. The Resolution resolves that, at a minimum, federal Internet gaming legislation must incorporate the following fundamental principles:

- Indian tribes are sovereign governments with a right to operate, regulate, tax, and license Internet gaming, and those rights must not be subordinated to any non-federal authority.

All federally recognized Indian tribes must be eligible to both operate and regulate Internet gaming. IGRA authorizes tribes to both operate and regulate brick and mortar casinos. The current regulatory/operation system in place for Indian gaming is working. For more than two decades, tribes have worked with the National Indian Gaming Commission (NIGC) to ensure the integrity of tribal games and protect tribal gaming revenue. A similar system is in place for state governments to both operate and regulate lottery systems. However, state lotteries do not have the added oversight of a federal regulatory agency.

In addition, if a federal regulatory system is developed and mandated, tribal governments ask that the NIGC be vested with authority to regulate tribal Internet gaming. IGRA established the NIGC as the principal federal regulatory body to oversee Indian gaming. Today, the NIGC is the only federal agency with experience in regulating any form of gaming in the United States. This provision should not supersede tribal governments' rights to regulate Internet gaming.

- Internet gaming authorized by Indian tribes must be available to customers in any locale where Internet gaming is not criminally prohibited.

Internet gaming transcends borders. Thus, Internet gaming legislation must acknowledge that customers may access tribal government operated and regulated Internet gaming sites as long as Internet gaming is not criminally prohibited where the eligible customer is located. Such acknowledgment would be consistent with current law and would recognize significant experience on the part of tribes in using technology to conduct gaming across borders.

IGRA specifically acknowledges Congress' intent that tribal gaming operations benefit from growing technology, with the intent of authorizing tribes to provide games to a broader audience. For more than two decades, tribes have conducted gaming beyond local tribal borders and across state borders by linking class II and class III machines to broaden participation in tribally regulated games. New federal legislation should embrace the expertise that tribes have built through IGRA.

Past statements of the U.S. Department of Justice support this position. ''[T]o the extent that any legislation would seek to exempt from its prohibition bets and wagers that are authorized by both the state or country in which the bettor and the recipient reside . Indian Tribes should be treated as every other sovereign for the purpose of authorizing gaming activity on their lands.'' *Statement of Kevin V. DiGregory, Deputy Assistant Attorney General, Criminal Division, http://www.justice.gov/criminal/cybercrime/kvd0698.htm.*

- Consistent with long-held federal law and policy, tribal Internet gaming revenues must not be subject to tax.

It's a fundamental principle of law that governments do not tax the essential revenues of other governments. The U.S. Constitution recognizes that Indian tribes are governments. Thus, Internet gaming legislation must acknowledge that tribal government Internet gaming revenues are not subject to taxation. Tribes are willing to maintain the same limits on the use of tribal Internet gaming revenue as are included in IGRA for the use of Indian gaming revenue. IGRA requires that tribes spend gaming revenues on five listed public purposes: tribal government operations, general welfare of the tribe and its members, economic development, donations to charitable organizations, and operations of nearby local governments. 25 U.S.C. 2710(b)(2)(B). This provision essentially assesses a 100 percent tribal tax on Indian gaming revenue. As a result tribal revenues are 100 percent dedicated to addressing the severe unmet needs of tribal communities. There is simply no room for federal or state taxation.

- Existing tribal government rights under Tribal-State Compacts and IGRA must be respected.

Tribal governments have invested significant resources in their operations based on the rights acknowledge under IGRA and in carefully negotiated tribal-state class III gaming compacts. These agreements must not be violated.

In addition, Internet gaming legislation must permit Indian tribes to operate Internet gaming without renegotiating existing tribal-state compacts. By legalizing Internet gaming, Congress will be establishing new law for a new industry. As noted above, Internet gaming transcends borders. Thus, tribes should be permitted to offer Internet gaming to consumers anywhere it is deemed legal by the government of jurisdiction. This position makes added sense in the case of Internet poker. Poker is considered a non-banked card game that would be considered class II gaming under IGRA in many cases, and thus, not subject to compacting requirements. Other arguments are being made that poker is a game of skill, not chance, and again likely outside the scope of compacting requirements.

- The legislation must not open up IGRA for amendments.

For hundreds of tribal governments there is simply too much at stake to open the Indian Gaming Regulatory Act up to amendments on the floor of either the House or Senate. Tribes have consistently opposed subjecting IGRA to amendments for the past 23 years. Many federal laws outside of Title 25 acknowledge the governmental status of Indian tribes. Thus, instead of amending IGRA, tribal governments ask that the principles included in the NIGA Resolution be followed as part of new legislation to authorize Internet gaming in the United States.

- Federal legalization of Internet gaming must provide positive economic benefits for Indian country.

This principle requires the United States to acknowledge its Constitutional, treaty and trust obligations to Indian tribes as well as the significant stake that tribal governments have in the existing gaming industry. To meet this principle, federal legislation legalizing Internet gaming must set-aside and dedicate funding to meet the significant unmet needs of tribal communities.

As noted above, tribal governments ceded and had taken hundreds of millions of acres of tribal homelands to help build this Nation. In return, the U.S. promised to provide for the education, health, safety and welfare of Indian people. These solemn promises have not been kept. Too many of our people continue to live with disease and poverty. Indian health care is substandard, violent crime is multiple times the national average, and unemployment on Indian reservations nationwide averages 50 percent. Tribal youth are among the most disadvantaged population in America. Our youth suffer the highest dropout rates and lowest education achievement levels in the Nation. The suicide rate for Native teens is 3.5 times the national average. Many tribal governments are using revenue generated from Indian gaming to address these severe unmet needs.

Economic studies show that legalized Internet gaming in the United States will adversely impact brick and mortar casinos, which in turn will impact the ability of tribes to meet their communities' needs. As a result, tribal governments ask that legislation legalizing Internet gaming in the U.S. be accompanied by a program set-aside to meet the government's treaty and trust obligations to Indian country.

Current Internet Legalization Proposals Before Congress

As noted above, Internet gaming bills that have been introduced in the House of Representatives in the 112th Congress (H.R. 1174 and H.R. 2366) as well as recent drafts developed in the Senate violate many of the principles discussed above. NIGA strongly opposes these proposals unless they are amended to adhere to the principles detailed in this testimony. The discussion below details some of the specific concerns that we have with the current proposals to legalize Internet gaming.

Commercial v. Government Internet Gaming

Current Internet gaming bills and drafts violate the first principle that all federally recognized Indian tribes should be eligible to both operate and regulate Internet gaming if such activity is legalized in the United States.

Current proposals envision only commercially operated Internet gaming, and ignore the ability of Indian tribes to operate Internet gaming sites as governmental entities. The bills would prohibit tribal governments from regulating Internet poker if the tribe also has a significant ownership interest in an Internet poker licensee— or is itself an operator.

Just as state governments have regulated state lottery systems for decades, tribal governments for more than two decades under IGRA, and even prior to IGRA, have established independent regulatory agencies that provide the day-to-day oversight of the games offered at tribal operations and of Indian gaming revenues. No one has a greater vested interest in ensuring the credibility of tribal games or protecting Indian gaming revenues than tribal governments. In 2010 alone, tribes spent $375 million on regulation. Our regulatory personnel include top law enforcement officials from tribal, federal, and state agencies. Tribes also employ state of the art surveillance and related technology, as well as the personnel educated and trained to manage this equipment. The expertise that our regulators have developed should be embraced in legislation to legalize Internet gaming in the United States.

Another significant concern with current bills is that they would skew the playing field to enable a few select most-favored regulators and operators to enter the field prior to other entities. Congress should not be in the business of picking and choosing winners and losers if or when it decides to establish a new industry such as Internet gaming. Carving out exemptions for certain states or certain gaming operators is unacceptable.

NIGC as Regulator of Tribal Internet Gaming

The current bills and drafts violate the principle that if a federal regulatory system is established that tribal governments continue to work with the National Indian Gaming Commission (NIGC). Current bills would subject tribal governments that are eligible to operate Internet gaming to the regulatory authority of either the Commerce or Treasury Departments. They also envision tribes working with a newly established Office of Internet Poker. These agencies, while striving to better understand tribal governments and the federal government's trust and treaty obligations towards tribes in recent years, do not have the longstanding relationship or understanding held between tribes and the NIGC and the Department of the Interior. The Interior Department has long been viewed as the point agency responsible for upholding the federal government's obligations to tribal governments. Again, the NIGC is the only federal agency with experience in regulating any form of gaming.

Tribal Government Revenues and Taxation

Current Internet gaming bills and recent drafts violate the principle that tribal Internet gaming revenues not be subject to taxation. Current bills would either place an across the board tax on Internet gaming revenues or place a flat licensing fee on tribal governments based on a percentage of Internet gaming revenues. Again, current bills envision only commercially operated Internet gaming, and do not acknowledge Indian tribes as governments. These provisions must be amended to acknowledge tribal Internet gaming revenue as that will be 100 percent dedicated to rebuilding tribal communities. Such governmental revenue should not be subject to taxation by another government.

Tribal Rights Under IGRA and in Existing Gaming Compacts

Current Internet bills also contain provisions that would violate the principles to preserve existing tribal rights under IGRA and in existing tribal-state gaming compacts. Some of these bills contain provisions under the heading ''No Impact on the Indian Gaming Regulatory Act.'' The title of the provision is misleading, as it would authorize the violation of existing tribal-state compacts provisions, such as exclusivity agreements. Voiding existing contract rights, such as exclusivity agreements, without the consent of affected states and tribes may violate the Fifth Amendment Due Process and Takings Clauses. The provision would also permit violation of IGRA's requirements for tribal eligibility to conduct gaming. For example, a state such as Utah, which criminally prohibits all forms of gambling, could authorize Internet gaming, but under this provision, such authorization would not affect the right of tribes within the state to conduct gaming under IGRA. These provisions should be amended to affirmatively recognize the full force and effect of existing tribal-state compact agreements as well as safeguard existing tribal government rights under IGRA.

Internet Gambling and the Deficit Reduction Plan

Proponents of legalizing Internet gaming have asked the Joint Select Committee on Deficit Reduction to include Internet gaming as part of the national strategy to cut the federal deficit. We strongly oppose inclusion of Internet gaming legalization as part of the national plan to reduce the federal deficit.

Legalization of Internet gaming is a controversial policy issue that must be carefully examined. As noted above, current House proposals to legalize Internet gaming have not been vetted by their respective committees and are not ready to be passed in the House of Representatives. In the Senate, no legislation has even been introduced in the 112th Congress.

However, if any attempts are made to insert Internet gaming legislation as part of the Deficit Reduction Plan, we urge this Committee to work with the members of the Joint Select Committee on Deficit Reduction to include the principles discussed in this testimony before permitting such a proposal to move forward.

Conclusion

For four decades, Indian gaming has proven to be the most effective tool for many tribes to begin to address generations of federal policies that sought to destroy tribal land holdings, culture, and economies. Many tribal governments are justly concerned that legalizing Internet gaming in the United States will threaten the American jobs and precious tribal government revenues established through Indian gaming.

To address these concerns, tribal governments ask that if federal Internet gaming legalization moves forward, that the legislation: (1) acknowledge that all federally recognized tribes are eligible, as governments not subject to taxation, to participate in the new industry as both operators and regulators; (2) that tribal Internet operations be open to customers wherever legal; (3) that the legislation fully protect tribal government rights under IGRA and existing tribal-state compacts; (4) that IGRA not be opened to amendment; and (5) that the legislation set-aside positive economic benefits to address the significant unmet needs of Indian country.

I again thank you for this opportunity to testify today. I look forward to working with the Committee on this important issue, and welcome any questions.

The CHAIRMAN. Thank you very much for your responses, Mr. Stevens.

Mr. D'Amato, will you please proceed with your testimony?

STATEMENT OF HON. ALFONSE D'AMATO, CHAIRMAN, THE POKER PLAYERS ALLIANCE; ACCOMPANIED BY JOHN PAPPAS, EXECUTIVE DIRECTOR, THE POKER PLAYERS ALLIANCE

Mr. D'AMATO. Thank you very much, Mr. Chairman. It is a pleasure to be here before you and see you again, and Vice Chairman Barrasso and Senator Udall.

Mr. Chairman, I am going to ask that my written remarks be entertained by the Committee as read in its entirety.

The CHAIRMAN. Without objection, that will be entered into the record.

Senator D'Amato. At the outset, Mr. Chairman, let me commend you for this important hearing. I am pleased to have the opportunity to testify as Chairman of the Poker Players Alliance. We represent 1,200,000 members who play this great game and great pastime of poker. I would like to at the outset say that we associate ourselves, the PPA, with those remarks and the testimony submitted, by Mr. Bozsum, the Chairman of the Mohegan Tribe. I did not see his testimony before. We did not prepare it together, either behind the scenes or in front. And I found there to be some tremendously comprehensive suggestions as to how to move forward.

First of all, we don't intend in the legislative process to open up the Internet to gaming as such, but rather for poker. The bills we support, the legislation such as Congressman Barton's, is for poker only. This will not have the kind of devastating impact, for example, that Vice Chairman Gobin is legitimately concerned with. What will the impact of the Internet, if you open it up to gambling, have on the brick and mortar facilities? By the way, what will the impact be if we legalize poker?

Right now only 1 percent of all of the revenues of games at Indian casinos comes from the poker tables. And as a matter of fact, we have empirical evidence that demonstrates since we have had, I want to say the sign of TV craze for Texas Hold'em on television, and since the Internet has been used by offshore companies, the revenues in the card rooms in brick and mortar have gone up, for both Indian casinos and those traditional brick and mortar on-Indian casinos. It has encouraged participation. So it is not a revenue loser.

Let me say we are losing revenues, vast sums. There are thousands of people who are employed offshore. And they are employed in providing Internet services to the United States. Many of them now are down in the islands, dozens and dozens of them. So now we have Americans playing on the Internet, and you cannot stop them, it is simply a check that they write and they send offshore. And there are no protections. They are limited. We don't have the kinds of consumer protections that we should, that exist in 80 other countries, but do not exist in many situations. And we saw a shocking situation where $150 million of poker players' money was improperly distributed by a so-called reputable company operating offshore. That is why there is a crying need to have the kind of Federal intervention to see to it that consumers are protected.

With respect to the Indian nations and their sovereignty, et cetera, let me make one thing very certain. And it is in my written testimony. I will refer to it. No Tribe, and I say this to the Chief and to all here, should be renegotiated, should require a renegotiation of a compact with a State as a condition of becoming a licensor and operator or otherwise participate in an Internet poker licensing regimen. No Tribe. You don't go back and say, we are going to alter your compact if you want to. We don't suggest that.

And indeed as it relates to some of the more contentious issues, if we sit down we can work them out. The question of taxing revenues, we are not looking to come and tax revenues at the site. The question of participation and who can and who should, the fact of the matter is that we believe that there are Indian Tribes today that have the sophistication in pooling together that can more than adequately compete. You mean to tell me if the Mohegans and the Oneidas got together, they could compete with any casino.

So this business of saying it will be unfair, what is unfair today is the total lack of supervision and regulations. The American consumers are entitled to it. And they are entitled to legislation that will deal with now what is a problem, totally unregulated poker playing on the Internet, other gambling games on the Internet.

I know you will have other questions, and I am ready to address them. And my time, I have gone 23 seconds over, but after all, I was a former member of the Senate. And Senator, if might share publicly one of our experiences together, I kept the Chairman up all night long in an 18-hour filibuster when he was in the Chair.

[Laughter.]

Mr. D'AMATO. Thank you, Mr. Chairman.

[The prepared statement of Mr. D'Amato follows:]

PREPARED STATEMENT OF HON. ALFONSE D'AMATO, CHAIRMAN, POKER PLAYERS ALLIANCE

Chairman Akaka and Members of the Committee, I am pleased to have this opportunity to testify before you today on the challenges and opportunities that licensed Internet poker would present for Tribal Governments. I am here in my role as Chairman of the Poker Players Alliance, an organization of 1.2 million Americans who like to play a great American game in casinos, in their homes, in bars, in charitable games and on the Internet. They do so for recreation, for camaraderie, for intellectual challenge and stimulation, and some of them do it for a living.

The PPA has been at the forefront of advocating for U.S. licensing and regulation of Internet poker for more than five years. Every year, millions of Americans play poker on the Internet on offshore sites licensed by foreign government, with varying degrees of consumer protection. No U.S. federal law and few state laws make it illegal for Americans to play poker on the Internet; when a prohibition does it exist it generally applies to the person receiving the wager—the operator of an Internet gaming site. Even today an American with a checking account and a high-speed Internet connection can deposit money on an offshore account and play poker, gamble on casino games, bet on sports and wager on horse races. What Americans cannot do is play Internet poker on a site that is licensed and regulated in the U.S., that creates jobs for American workers, or that provides revenue for federal, state and of course tribal governments. It is well-past time for Congress to change that, and there are efforts underway, particularly in the U.S. House of Representatives, to do so.

In evaluating the implications of Internet gaming for Indian Country, I would commend to the Committee's attention a white paper commissioned by the National Indian Gaming Association entitled ''Internet Gambling Developments in International Jurisdictions: Insight for Indian Nations.

The study notes that regulation of Internet gaming and Internet poker is not a groundbreaking endeavor. While the U.S. may be well behind the curve, regulation of this activity has been ongoing for several years throughout Europe and other parts of the world; in fact nearly 80 jurisdictions have regulated Internet gambling. Through appropriate regulation and oversight, countries like the United Kingdom, Denmark, France, Italy, Belgium and Australia are providing their citizens with strong consumer protections and they are also reaping the economic benefits. A *New York Times*[1] story reported on the positive economic impact regulated online gambling has had on economies throughout the European Union.

Today, Internet gambling is an estimated 30 billion dollar global industry. In 2010, it was estimated that revenues generated from U.S. players was roughly 6 billion dollars. A recent economic impact study examined the potential of a U.S. regulated market and revealed that it would yield more than 30,000 new jobs and tens of billions in tax revenue and economic activity for the United States. Today, each and every dollar and job created by this industry is being done to the benefit to other countries and not the United States and not our nation's Indian tribes.

As I understand it, the purpose of this hearing is not to decide whether or not Congress should pass poker licensing legislation; rather, it is to identify where the interests of Indian Country lie with respect to such legislation, and how Tribal governments and Tribal gaming enterprises might participate in a licensed Internet poker or Internet gaming market. I will focus my testimony accordingly.

In discussing these questions, I would begin with a categorical statement: The Poker Players Alliance believes that Indian Country should be substantial players in a regulated U.S. market. We would like to see Tribal governments as federally-recognized licensing bodies. We would like to see Tribal gaming enterprises as licensed operators, as well as affiliates and network partners for other licensed operators. In the poker marketplace, PPA speaks for the consumers, and competition is always good for consumers.

Models of Federal Internet poker regulatory structures are still in flux, but for discussion purposes, let us assume it looks something like what is proposed in H.R. 2366, Rep. Joe Barton's Internet poker bill. Under that bill, state and tribal governments that want to license Internet gaming must apply to the U.S. Department of Commerce for recognition as a qualified licensing body. Commerce would issue a set of regulations delineating what state and tribal licensing programs must contain. Once a particular jurisdiction's licensing program is certified by Commerce, that jurisdiction can begin issuing licenses, and any licensee of a recognized jurisdiction could accept Internet poker play from any state or tribe that had not opted out of the federal system. State and tribal governments could opt-out of the federal system by having their chief executive notify the Secretary of Commerce of their intent to opt-out; licensees would be prohibited from accepting play from any jurisdiction that had opted out. Finally, Tribal governments could participate as licensors, and tribal gaming enterprises could participate as licensees, but Tribal governments would not be allowed to license their own gaming enterprises to take play from off of the reservation.

As you all know very well, the central construct upon which Indian gaming is built is the principle of geographic sovereignty—the fact that federally-recognized

---

[1] Europe Unleashes Online Gambling to Fill Coffers. *New Yorks Times*, July 27, 2010.

tribal governments have the right to govern the actions of people and businesses on their reservation land, with little or no interference from federal and state governments. This principle has allowed many Indian tribes to use casino gaming as a substantial tool for economic development.

Certain entrepreneurial tribes have used the proceeds of their successful gaming operations to invest in assets—both gaming and non-gaming—outside their reservation. Examples of this include the Seminoles' acquisition of the Hard Rock chain, and the investment of the Mashantucket Pequot tribe in a casino in Pennsylvania. In these cases, the relevant Tribe's business enterprise submitted to taxation and regulation from the jurisdiction in which the facility was located.

The challenge posed by Internet gaming is this: under established U.S. law, an Internet wager transaction occurs in two places—the location of the merchant server and the location of the player's computer. This dual jurisdiction will produce some serious policy questions, and I appreciate this committee's interest in addressing them. PPA has staked out several positions on some of these issues, and I would like to briefly state them here.

If federal Internet poker legislation is enacted, we believe it should make clear that participation by state governments, Tribal governments, state-licensed entities or tribally licensed entities does not affect the prerogatives of states or tribes under the Indian Gaming Regulatory Act. The decision of a tribal government to become a licensor or a tribal gaming enterprise to become a licensee should not require re-negotiation of a Class III compact. The decision of a state without commercial casino gaming to license Internet poker or to not opt-out of a federal system should not turn that state into a Class III state for IGRA purposes. The IGRA Class III compacting system was designed to deal with the geographic proximity between states and gaming tribes. On the Internet, geographic proximity is meaningless, and under every proposed bill, states and tribes have the right to opt-out of Internet poker.

Another issue is the question of taxation of Internet poker. As we understand it, the question of whether poker licensing legislation will include new tax provisions has not been resolved. Naturally, those taxes paid in the ordinary course of doing business will apply—for example, players paying taxes on their winnings—but we are told that no decision has been made as to whether there will be additional tax provisions as have been proposed in previous drafts.

If tax provisions are included in a licensing bill, the PPA is optimistic that creative minds could structure an Internet tax regime that could be acceptable to all sides. Such a regime would avoid breaching the principle that Indian gaming is not subject to taxation, but that also avoids providing tribal gaming an unfair competitive advantage in the marketplace.

A similar issue arises around the question of regulation of Internet gaming by Tribal gaming commissions. I think the position of the commercial gaming industry is that tribes can be licensors or licensees, but that they cannot license themselves to take play from off of the reservation. Indian Country has been clear that they would oppose any regime that would subject tribal gaming to non-federal regulation. Many in Congress are at least very skeptical of—if not outright opposed to—the idea of creating a new federal bureaucracy to license and regulate Internet gaming. Certainly, the NIGC does not currently have the staff, the resources or the expertise to do so. One possible solution would be for one tribe or a consortium of tribes to become sort of a super-regulator for the rest of Indian country.

Some drafts of Internet gaming legislation have given preference to certain state gaming authorities over other state and tribal gaming commissions, based on those states' history of regulating gaming, or the size of their regulated industry. PPA understands the desire on the part of Internet poker proponents to avoid a ''race to the bottom,'' where a particular regulator uses lax regulation to attract licensees, and to advantage those licensees in the marketplace. However, rather than having legislation pre-judge who will be the best regulator, we believe that the federal agency certifying state programs should evaluate each proposed regime on its merits. Those state and tribal gaming authorities who propose the most comprehensive and rigorous regulatory programs should be the ones recognized first.

Finally, the National Indian Gaming Association has taken the position that Internet gaming legislation should provide net benefits to Indian Country. Today, Internet poker is a multi-billion dollar industry that is entirely offshore. By bringing that industry on-shore and allowing tribes to participate, it is difficult to see how such legislation could fail to benefit Indian Country. Concerns that licensed Internet poker will cannibalize tribal brick-and-mortar gaming are simply misplaced. First of all, the overwhelming majority of tribal brick-and-mortar gaming is slots and house-banked table games. While some tribes may have poker rooms, poker is a very small percentage of tribal gaming revenue. Poker players and slot players are very different people. Second, Internet poker has been around for almost ten years—any competitive impacts would already have been felt.

I would like to highlight, however, one developing situation which may have far-reaching consequences for tribal gaming. Several states are in the process of authorizing their state lotteries to sell virtual instant scratch-off tickets on the Internet. A scratch-off ticket on the Internet makes a computer work exactly like a slot machine: A player deposits money into a playing account, they buy one "ticket", and the software displays several values on the screen. If the values match up a certain way, the player wins; if they don't, the player plays again. As I mentioned before, the mainstay of Indian Gaming is slot machines. The benefit to Indian tribes of having slot machines will be significantly less if state lotteries are turning every computer in the country into a slot machine. If Indian Country is looking for a competitive threat to their core business, virtual scratch-off tickets are a far greater threat than regulated poker.

Mr. Chairman, I would again like to express my gratitude for this opportunity to testify, and I look forward to answering any questions Committee members may have.

The CHAIRMAN. Thank you very much for your testimony, Senator D'Amato. We are so glad you were able to be here.

Let me now call on Ms. Coleman. Please proceed with your testimony.

STATEMENT OF PENNY COLEMAN, PRINCIPAL, COLEMAN INDIAN LAW

Ms. COLEMAN. Thank you, Chairman, Vice Chairman. It is a pleasure. My name is Penny Coleman. I am the owner of Coleman Indian Law and in counsel to Anderson Indian Law. But my main claim to fame is that I was probably the longest-acting general counsel in the history of the Federal Government. From 1994 to 2010, I was the Chief Counsel at the NIGC, for the majority of the time I was there. So I was there when they started, I was there through last year. And it was excellent experience and helps inform my testimony today.

I did want to comment on a couple of things that were said, or were in the testimony before I go into mine. One is that there has been a lot of discussion about how should this legislation be prepared, if it is. It seems obviously that a fair and open discussion with the Tribal leaders is something that is absolutely necessary. If you have entities, if you have governments that have 43 percent of the gaming revenue, well, then, their voice must count, especially when you consider where they have come from, what they have been able to develop over the last 25 years of gaming.

In addition, with respect to whether there has to be change in IGRA, no, not really. You can do legislation without changing the Indian Gaming Regulatory Act. You have to be careful on how you do it. But the NIGC is responsible for Internet gaming on Indian lands. Obviously there is going to have to be some changes with respect to jurisdictional roles and jurisdiction situations where the States and the Federal Governments and the Tribes are all going to have to work together because of the fact that Internet gaming would be, under Federal legislation, would be nationwide.

And I think I need to emphasize the fact that when you are looking at the Tribal nations, you are not talking about commercial gaming, you are talking about government gaming. And Tribal governments, just like State governments, State governments run lotteries. That is government gaming. No one wants to disturb that government gaming. Nobody suggests that States can't own and regulate lotteries.

Well, there is no reason to suggest that Indian nations can't own and regulate Internet gaming. It is the same thing. And it is not unfair to commercial gaming, because commercial gaming and government gaming are two different things. And that is something I think that really needs to be remembered.

But with respect to the legislation that I have seen, the draft bills and the bills that have been sponsored, the concern that I have is that if there aren't some major changes, there are many Tribe that are simply going to be run over. There are Indian nations, like Mohegan and others who are ready to go. They know exactly what they are going to do and how they are going to do it.

But others are, they now it is only a possibility. And they need to spend their time and their money supporting their government programs and not chasing after something that may or may not happen. So they have reflected that it is not quite yet on their radar, they haven't been asked to comment on specific legislation. They don't know, they are not ready to spin their wheels on this. They are the ones that are going to be run over, they are the ones that are not going to have an opportunity if the bills that are out there are passed. The ones that say that only the States of New Jersey and Nevada are going to be the regulators, well, if those two States have the lock on the regulation, what is going to happen to the Tribes as regulators? By the time they get in there, they get licensed, it is going to be too late for them. And it would take a long time.

The Department of Commerce would take years to get to the point where they could actually license someone. The NIGC's experience, which Mr. Roberts already discussed at some length, is a good example of how long it takes. You have to let the people appointed, you have to develop regulations, you have to learn who your constituency is, you have to figure out what the best practices are. And the Department of Commerce, it would take years to do it.

The NIGC actually has some benefits, because of the Indian Gaming Regulatory Act, they can hire and pass regulations a lot more quickly than most Federal agencies, because of some things that are in the Act.

I think it is really necessary that we have Federal legislation. We have to make clear that the Wire Act doesn't apply, work out the jurisdictional issues. It is necessary that Tribes have the opportunity to opt in or opt out, that they not be limited by the States' decisions. Because they do have their own land, they shouldn't be limited, when you are talking about a nationwide Internet gaming.

And it is extremely important that Tribes not be subject to outside taxation. They are already putting their money to government programs, to charities, to local communities. They are not using the money for million dollar CEOs. They are using the money for their government programs.

The decisions that Tribes have to make are numerous. If this legislation is passed, you have to give them an opportunity to be looking at that if you are going to go forward with regulation.

This concludes my testimony. I apologize for taking longer than I was supposed to.

[The prepared statement of Ms. Coleman follows:]

PREPARED STATEMENT OF PENNY COLEMAN, PRINCIPAL, COLEMAN INDIAN LAW

Chairman, Vice Chairman, Committee members and other distinguished participants:

Thank you for inviting me to speak to the Committee today.

My name is Penny Coleman. I am the owner of Coleman Indian Law and serve as counsel to Anderson Indian Law, both of which represent Tribal Nations. In 2010 I retired from the Federal Government. During my career, I worked on Indian gaming issues for over 20 years and served as chief counsel for many of my 16 years at the National Indian Gaming Commission (NIGC).

I am here today to discuss some of the challenges and impacts of Internet gaming on Indian Nations if legislation was passed now.

I cannot emphasize enough that, without legislation that considers and mitigates the impacts of Internet gaming on tribal government gaming, many of the Indian Nations will simply be run over. Most of the draft legislation limits tribal participation by making eligibility to operate or regulate Internet gaming unnecessarily restrictive. Most Indian Nations would not qualify. Further, such legislation assumes that Indian Nations cannot both own and regulate Internet gaming while still recognizing that States own and regulate lotteries.

There are many Nations poised to operate and regulate Internet gaming. There is a large consortium of Nations and card rooms in California that is already operating a free play poker site as a precursor to its planned Internet gaming. A few other nations are operating similar on-line, free play sites. Many Nations, however, have not had the time or money to turn to Internet gaming while it remains only a possibility rather than a certainty. For many, Internet gaming is not yet on their radar.

The National Indian Gaming Association laid out several basic principles its tribal constituents require to assure that Internet gaming is good for the Nations rather than a detriment. One important principle is the concept that Internet gaming should result in positive economic benefits for the Indian Nations.

For the Nations, historically mired in poverty, it is of utmost importance that Internet gaming does not take away the positive economic benefits that gaming now brings to them. Internet gaming offers Tribal Nations the opportunity to develop a new industry that can complement their brick and mortar facilities. Las Vegas and New Jersey recognize this potential and are already developing online sites that would tie into their existing player's club databases. If Tribal Nations are not included in authorizing legislation, we can expect that fewer dollars will be spent at the Tribal Nations facilities. Indian Country also needs legislation that will place all Tribes in a position to benefit from Internet gaming, even those, or especially those, in isolated parts of the country.

The draft bills limit Tribes opportunity to engage immediately in Internet gaming while assuring that a few States can do so. This lack of parity assures that many Tribes will completely miss the Internet gaming opportunities. By the time regulations are developed and tribal applications processed, potential patrons will already have identified their favorite gaming sites. Within a short time, we can expect that there will be a handful of gaming sites that will bring in the largest number of gamers and all the rest will be an afterthought.

Designating the Department of Commerce as the regulatory oversight agency for Indian Internet gaming will not resolve those problems. And it will definitely not assure that Tribes can quickly become competitors in Internet gaming.

The National Indian Gaming Commission is the best example of the challenges the Department of Commerce would face in the first years of its existence. From 1988 to the issuance of the NIGC regulations in early 1993, there were four years where the federal government simply did not provide any gaming oversight. It took two years before the first chairman was appointed and two years to appoint staff and issue regulations. NIGC then had to organize, train, and add staff and regional offices while developing its own expertise in Indian gaming.

While developing its own infrastructure and expertise, the NIGC developed working relationships with over 200 tribal governments and over 200 tribal gaming commissions. NIGC staff had to understand and appreciate the cultural backgrounds and economic challenges facing each Nation and develop regulatory and training programs that would serve the Nations' needs. The NIGC's early efforts at conducting background checks and assisting the Nations on criminal history checks were time consuming and impractical. Employees would have already moved on before these checks were done. It had to work with the Tribes, the FBI and finally OPM to develop an investigatory program that really worked.

Fortunately, IGRA provides some relief from the usual federal bureaucratic impediments that slow federal agencies. The NIGC is exempt from some of the appointment, classification and pay restrictions imposed on other agencies. This allows the NIGC to hire more quickly and determine pay based on its needs. Consequently, the NIGC can compete to a limited extent with the Nations and companies which are also hiring gaming talent. The NIGC, because of its status as an independent agency, is also able to publish regulations more quickly.

The Department of Commerce will have none of these advantages. They will not know Indian Nations or gaming. They will not bring regulatory or enforcement experience or even much Internet experience to the system. Consequently, they will delay tribal opportunity in Internet gaming for years. I attached an article to my testimony that describes this issue in more detail.

Further, the draft bills do not take into consideration the need to assure that tribal brick and mortar facilities are not negatively impacted, to assure that Tribes are placed at least on equal footing with the States, and that profits from Internet gaming are not diverted away from tribal government services. Taxing the Nations establishes a bad precedent for Tribes and is really unnecessary. The Tribal Nations have been completely willing to pay for the cost of federal oversight as well as pay for the cost of the day to day regulation of their gaming. There are other mechanisms, such as that established under the Indian Gaming Regulatory Act (IGRA), which allow Tribes to pay for regulating costs without being subjected to taxation.

Tribes, like States, should be able to opt in or out of Internet gaming and not be limited by the decisions of the State that surrounds them. To compete, Tribes need to be able to offer Internet gaming wherever it is legally operated in the United States. This also allows all Tribal Nations to compete in the same manner as the States as well as other Tribes.

To have nationwide competition, federal legislation is necessary. Although states could individually authorize Internet gaming, jurisdictional, regulatory and enforcement questions would quickly arise between the States and Tribal Nations when offering gaming outside the individual State's borders. Such legislation could also resolve whether the Wire Act applies to Internet gaming.

If the IGRA taught us anything, making tribal government Internet gaming operations subject to state law and regulation, especially without the Nations' ready agreement, will cause ongoing conflict and litigation. Under IGRA, some states adopted a policy of overreaching and the view that Indian gaming should financially benefit them. They failed to recognize that they were working with another sovereign government and treated the Nations as commercial establishments rather than governments with program and infrastructure needs. This approach resulted in continued litigation, gaming not sanctioned by IGRA and some Nations unable to game because States were able to use the 11th Amendment as a shield against litigation. They failed to recognize Indian gaming as legitimate governmental gaming in the same manner as state lotteries are governmental gaming. I do not mean to suggest that this was the experience of all Tribal Nations. Certainly many describe very positive relationships with state governments. However, the conflicts have been often and severe enough that I urge Congress to look very closely at any legislation before subordinating tribal government interests to state interests.

IGRA also assumed that the States were in the best position to regulate gaming. This quickly proved to be a false assumption. Many states did not have regulatory infrastructures, knowledge and experience in gaming and were unwilling or unable to develop the day to day capabilities for regulating. They often did not understand the cultural and governmental differences between States and Tribal Nations or the economic challenges facing the Nations. We cannot expect these issues to disappear under new Internet legislation.

The draft bills raise other questions. For example, they do not prohibit cyber cafes. Cyber cafes could pop up all over serving as strong competitors to the established brick and mortar facilities. Cyber cafes could also allow a slot type gaming experience and allow pay offs on the premises. The result would be small casinos that technically meet the requirements of the Internet gaming laws while directly competing with brick and mortar casinos.

Finally, the Nations will need to make a number of decisions before they launch Internet gaming. Will it operate or regulate Internet gaming? Or, if permitted, will it do both? What is the best way to assure that the Tribal Nations will profit from Internet gaming? Who will it work with -other Tribes, established consortia, established gaming companies, or newcomers, such as Amazon or Facebook, that have tremendous lists of potential clients? Who should finance the endeavor and how should it be regulated? What are the best practices for regulation? What kinds of cross jurisdictional agreements are needed and can be reached to assure that the gaming, minors, and patrons are protected? Can a Tribe afford not to go on line? What kind of tie in should there be with the Nation's brick and mortar facility. These decisions are complex and numerous. Many of the Tribal Nations are only just starting to answer these questions.

While there is much more that could be said on this important issue, this concludes my remarks. I thank the Committee Members for the opportunity to provide my views. If you have any questions, I stand ready to answer them.

Attachment

CAN THE NIGC OVERSEE INTERNET GAMING?

by Penny Coleman—*Indian Gaming* September 2011

As the availability of Internet poker in the United States becomes more inevitable than just possible, many are looking to theNational Indian Gaming Commission (NIGC) to oversee the tribal nations' participation in Internet gaming. So, is this a task that the NIGC can handle? Most definitely. It is the only federal agency that can. The NIGC has two areas of expertise that lend itself to regulation of tribal gaming. First, it knows Indian Nations. Second, it knows gaming. In addition, the NIGC is in a position to establish a regulatory structure much more quickly and efficiently than any other federal agency.

In the twenty years that the NIGC has operated, it fostered a working relationship with over 200 gaming tribes. To do so, it developed a constantly updated listing of government and regulatory leaders, a data base of gaming sites and the Indian lands they occupy, a working relationship with tribal leaders and employees, and a regulatory and training program designed to assist each Nation with its regulatory issues. To make that program effective, NIGC leadership and staff had to understand the cultural backgrounds and economic challenges of the Nations it oversees. Many brought that understanding with them to their positions; others had to learn through experience.

NIGC's experience in gaming regulation has no counterpart in the federal government.TheNIGCis specifically tasked with regulatory oversight of poker. It has 20 years of experience in all facets of gaming regulation. Such experience includes regulating linked games across tribal jurisdictions. On the other hand, while the Department of Defense has some experience in regulating gaming, that experience is limited and not centralized. Further, while the Department of Commerce is included in draft legislation as a potential regulator, that department has no regulatory enforcement experience, no gaming experience, limited experience with tribes, and experience with the Internet as a policy advisor rather than a regulator.

At this point, the NIGC can assume responsibility for Internet regulation faster and with fewer glitches than any other federal agency. From the passage of the Indian Gaming Regulatory Act in 1988 to the issuance of theNIGC's regulations, there were four years where the federal government failed to provide any kind of gaming oversight. The first two years were spent waiting for the appointment of the first chairman. The remaining two years required time to appoint staff and issue regulations. After those first four years, the NIGC organized internally, trained and added additional staff and regional offices, and expanded its own areas of expertise. It was many years before NIGC oversight was truly considered effective. Any federal agency taking on this task must take on the same development. Such a task takes time; a commodity that a new federal agency will not have.

The NIGC's freedom from a few of the usual bureaucratic impediments will help it progress quickly.TheNIGCis exempt from some of the burdensome appointment and constraining compensation requirements. These exemptions allow the agency to hire within weeks rather than the months federal agencies normally take. And, by being exempt from restrictive pay requirements, it can be more competitive with the many companies that will be seeking employees with Internet gaming expertise.The NIGC, by virtue of its size and independence from certain rulemaking requirements, can also promulgate regulations much more quickly than other agencies.

Further, the NIGC already has a system in place to conduct background checks of major gaming companies and employees and to assist tribes to do so. The NIGC serves as the conduit between the FBI and theNations seeking criminal history information. To do so, it moved from a manual finger printing system that took months to provide results to a nationwide electronic system that provides criminal history information to the Nations within minutes. It also established a section within the NIGC that carries out extensive background investigations with the assistance of the Office of Personnel Management.

Finally, the NIGC's requirement that two of the three commissioners are tribal members and its recent adoption of an Indian preference employment policy help assure that the NIGC is staffed with many who will not have to learn about Indian Nations to do their jobs. Employing people from the communities that are served is critical to the credibility of the agency and its ability to foster relationships built on trust. What's more, it confirms the federal government's commitment to the policy of promoting tribal economic development, self-sufficiency, and strong tribal governments.

Taken together, NIGC's experience, expertise and infrastructure make it the only agency for the job.

The CHAIRMAN. Thank you very much, Ms. Coleman.

Mr. Eve, will you please proceed with your testimony?

STATEMENT OF GRANT W. EVE, CPA, CFE, MANAGER, JOSEPH EVE

Mr. EVE. Good afternoon, Mr. Chairman, Mr. Vice Chairman. I send my regards to Senator Tester from my home State of Montana. I would like to thank you for the opportunity to testify today. It is an honor. I applaud the Committee for having this hearing on Internet gaming in an effort to find out the potential impact to Indian Tribes.

My name is Grant Eve, I work for Joseph Eve, a consulting and certified public accounting firm that works with over 100 Tribal entities each year. Prior to joining Joseph Eve, I worked with Deloitte LLP in Las Vegas, in the firm's national gaming practice. I worked with several Tribal and commercial casinos in this capacity.

Let me begin by saying Internet gaming today is a substantial industry, estimated to be generating approximately $30 billion worldwide. Some of this revenue is generated by illegal offshore organizations paying no tax to the countries they operate in. And some of this revenue is generated by licensed Internet gaming operators in jurisdictions like the U.K., Canada, Australia, Sweden and others where the activity is regulated.

Many analysts estimate the global gaming market to be in the range of $110 billion to $125 billion, excluding illegal operations. To put this in perspective, if conservative estimates are around $30 billion for online gaming and the global gaming market is estimated around $120 billion, one in $4 to $5 is gambled online today. Some analysts estimate worldwide Internet gaming revenue will increase at 10 to 15 percent or possibly more if it is legalized in the United States.

So in conclusion on this point I want to make, the brick and mortar casinos are either decreasing or breaking even, where Internet gaming revenue continue to grow unimpeded at double digit rates.

The impact on regulated Internet gaming on Indian gaming will depend significantly on the details of the legislation proposed. Whether it is at the State or Federal level hinges on many factors such as how the law will be written, what games will be legal, the eligibility of current Internet gaming operators, suppliers, vendors, marketers, the taxation structure, the eligibility of State lotteries, the eligibility of current brick and mortar gaming operators in the U.S. How and if the legislation will affect State compacts and/or IGRA, how Internet gaming operators would be governed, specifically as it applies to American Indian Tribes. And finally, State restrictions.

One of the more significant potential impacts on Indian gaming from Internet gaming is the extent to which Tribes would need to compete with commercial gaming. Big commercial gaming has nationally recognized brants, large capital resources and alliances with European Internet gaming operators. The vast majority of Tribes do not have the resources to compete against these would-be competitors if they were to operate independently.

Therefore, it is not surprising the Tribes are concerned that Internet gaming could take away resources from their brick and mortar efforts and put them on unequal footing. It only seems natural that should Internet gaming become legalized, that Indian Tribes should be allowed to operate, regulate, tax, host and license Internet gaming licensed websites as sovereign nations, no different than how the Tribes operate brick and mortar gaming today.

Regulation is a significant issue when you consider online gaming from Tribal operators. The regulators of Tribal brick and mortar facilities are the Tribal gaming agencies. Other regulators include the NIGC, the State in which the casino resides and the outside auditors. Not only does regulation ensure benefits to the customer, it also provides jobs. The Indian regulatory system employs more than 3,400 expert regulators and staff.

The issue of regulation needs to be addressed further when it comes to Internet gaming. With the maturity of the Internet, the increase in mobile network data speed and the advancement in device technology, it has changed the dynamics of the Internet gaming industry as a whole. Internet gaming is available today to anyone who has access to a computer and connection to the Internet. Anyone who is serious about gambling can find ways around the laws to gamble online today. The Senator mentioned being in your house and losing your house. People are doing that right today in the United States on unregulated sites.

If Internet gaming is legalized, Tribal operations are going to need an opportunity to build and capitalize on the market to protect self-sufficiency. Indian gaming has been the most successful benefit to the economic development within Indian Tribal communities. These funds have been used to improve health care, education, entrepreneurship and public safety in Indian Country.

While I agree with the statement on 1 percent that the Senator made, that doesn't mean that their spouse isn't playing a slot machine or that guy is going from a poker table to a table game.

Ultimately, I believe more information needs to be collected before a proper decision can be made. There is too much at risk for Indian Tribes to jeopardize what has been created since Congress enacted the Indian Gaming Regulatory Act in 1998.

Thank you for this opportunity. I look forward to answering any questions you may have.

[The prepared statement of Mr. Eve follows:]

PREPARED STATEMENT OF GRANT W. EVE, CPA, CFE, MANAGER, JOSEPH EVE

Good afternoon, Mr. Chairman and members of the Committee. I'd like to thank you for the opportunity to testify today, it is an honor. I applaud the committee for having this hearing on Internet gaming in an effort to find out the potential impact to Indian tribes.

My name is Grant Eve and I work for JOSEPH EVE, a consulting and certified public accounting firm that works with over 100 tribal entities each year. We specialize in Indian Country and have been working with tribes and casinos for over 25 years providing audit, accountings services, consulting, and internal control services. Prior to joining JOSEPH EVE, I worked with Deloitte LLP in the National Gaming Practice, in Las Vegas, Nevada. I worked with several tribal and commercial casinos in this capacity.

Summary of Testimony

My testimony today will provide a background on financial figures associated with brick and mortar casinos and internet gaming, potential impact of internet gaming to Indian tribes, regulation, unanswered questions and conclude with a brief summary.

Financial Figures

Let me begin by saying, Internet gaming today is a substantial industry, estimated to be generating approximately $30 billion dollars worldwide. Some of this revenue is generated by illegal, offshore organizations paying no tax to the countries they operate in and some of this revenue is generated by licensed internet gaming operators in jurisdictions like the United Kingdom, Canada, Australia, Sweden and others where the activity is regulated.

In the United States, we have almost 1,000 tribal and commercial, "land based" casinos operating across the country and many in the industry are trying to understand how and if, Internet gaming is affecting their gaming operations.

United States commercial gaming revenues have been steadily decreasing from the record high of $37.52 billion in 2007 to $34.60 billion in 2010. This represents a decrease of over 8% from 2007's record revenue numbers. This revenue estimate includes the states that allow commercial casino operations (non-tribal). The National Indian Gaming Commission reported Indian gaming revenues have remained unchanged between 2010 and 2009 at $26.5 billion. This revenue analysis includes over 422 independently audited financial statements from 236 gaming tribes in the United States.

Global gaming revenue figures are not as clear as U.S. gaming figures due to vague reporting requirements of various jurisdictions, little online gaming reporting requirements, the rapid expansion of Asia, and unreported illegal gambling enterprises. Many analysts estimate the global gaming market to be in the range of $110-125 billion excluding illegal operations. To put this into perspective, if conservative estimates of Internet gaming are about $30 billion and the global gaming market is estimated around $120 billion, one in every four dollars is gambled online. This ratio of worldwide Internet gaming revenues to land based gaming revenue is increasing as land based gaming revenue is decreasing in many regions of the world and Internet gaming revenue continues to increase. Some analysts' estimate worldwide Internet gaming revenue will increase at 10-15%, or possibly more, if it is legalized in the United States. Despite the high profile indictments of illegal internet gaming operators by the U.S. Department of Justice on April 15th, 2011, illegal Internet based betting and wagering continues today in the United States with unregulated providers and in places where the activity is currently regulated such as Canada and the United Kingdom.

In conclusion, brick and mortar casino revenues are decreasing or breaking even and internet gaming revenues continue to grow unimpeded

Potential Impact of Internet Gaming to Indian Gaming

The impact of regulated Internet Gaming on Indian gaming will depend significantly on the details of the legislation proposed, whether it is at the state or federal level. There have been many debates about the potential impact that Internet gaming might have on Indian gaming. Specifically, many tribal leaders feel that this could be detrimental to Indian gaming and others feel that this could be an opportunity for Indian gaming if tribes are strategically positioned when, and if, it is legalized.

The impact hinges on many factors, such as:

1. How the law will be written
    a. What games will be legal
    b. Eligibility of current Internet gaming operators, suppliers, vendors, marketers
    c. Taxation structure
    d. Eligibility of state lotteries
    e. Eligibility of current brick and mortar gaming operators in the U.S.
2. How and if the legislation will affect state-compacts and/or IGRA
3. How Internet gaming operators would be governed, specifically as it applies to American Indian tribes
4. State restrictions

Since poker generated revenue represents a very small portion of overall casino revenues in Indian country, legalization of Internet poker could represent an economic opportunity for the tribes to grow a business segment that traditionally has not been a significant one. According to JOSEPH EVE's 2011 Indian Gaming Cost of Doing Business Report © on the allocation of Indian Gaming revenue by segment, poker accounted for less than 1 % of revenues. The Indian Gaming Cost of Doing Business Report is a business management aid designed to benchmark casino financial performance with over 35 pages of useful data and metrics. The 2011 report (2010 fiscal year data) has financial information from over 75 Indian casinos.

One of the more significant potential impacts on Indian gaming from Internet gaming is the extent to which the tribes would need to compete with commercial gaming. Big commercial gaming has nationally recognized brands, large capital resources and alliances with European Internet gaming operators. The vast majority of tribes do not have the resources to compete against these would be competitors if they were to operate independently. Therefore it is not surprising that the tribes are concerned Internet gaming could take away resources from their brick and mortar efforts and put them on unequal footing with commercial competitors.

It would seem only natural that should Internet gaming become legalized that Indian tribes be allowed to operate, regulate, tax, host and license Internet gaming websites as sovereign nations, no different than how the tribes operate brick and mortar gaming today.

By combining online and offline club membership programs, tribal casinos could offer additional incentives to encourage Internet gamblers to visit their brick and mortar casinos and resorts. If tribes decided to work together in this area, the player would reap the benefits by accumulating incentives from tribal casinos across the country.

Regulation

Regulation is a significant issue when you consider online gaming for tribal operators. The regulator of tribal brick and mortar facilities are the tribal gaming agencies. Other regulators are the National Indian Gaming Commission, the state in which the casino resides, and the outside auditors. Not only does regulation ensure benefits to the customer, it also provides jobs. The Indian regulatory system employs more than 3,400 expert regulators and staff. This issue of regulation needs to be addressed further when it comes to Internet gaming.

Summary

The maturation of the Internet, the increase of mobile network data speed and the advancement in device technology has changed the dynamics of the gaming industry as a whole. Internet gaming is a relatively new form of gambling that customers demand today and they are willing to send their money overseas to prove it. While many experts deliberate over the true benefits of Internet gaming, other countries are taking advantage of the Internet gaming market. Some of the unknown questions that could define this industry in the United State include:

- What, if any, impact will regulated internet gaming have on land-based gaming?
- Will Internet gaming compliment land-based facilities and increase overall revenue?
- How will this affect "overall" revenue for Indian country?
- Who will be the regulators of tribal internet gaming?

Internet gaming is available today to anyone who has access to a computer and a connection to the internet. Anyone that is serious about gambling can find ways around the law to gamble online.

If Internet gaming is legalized, tribal operations are going to need an opportunity to build and capitalize on this market to protect self-sufficiency. Indian gaming has been the most successful benefit to the economic development within the Indian tribal communities. These funds have been used to improve health care, education and public safely in Indian country.

Ultimately, more information needs to be collected before a proper decision can be made. There is too much at risk for Indian tribes to jeopardize what has been created since Congress enacted Indian Gaming Regulatory Act in 1988.

Thank you for this opportunity and I look forward to answering any questions you may have.

The CHAIRMAN. Thank you very much, Mr. Eve, for your testimony.

Mr. Ernie Stevens, NIGA, Tribes and Tribal organizations, are opposed to taxing Tribal governments. If Internet gaming legislation is enacted, what mechanism should be used to fund the regulation of that industry?

Mr. STEVENS. I don't think that we are opposed to anything that is beyond what services are provided to the Tribes, as in the case with the NIGC. We understand what is fair. But taxation beyond that is inappropriate.

Mr. VAN NORMAN. Mr. Chairman, if I might?

The CHAIRMAN. Mr. Van Norman?

Mr. VAN NORMAN. The NIGC uses regulatory fees to raise revenue for their regulatory services. We do not object to a fee for regulatory services. What Tribal governments are saying is that we are funding the essential government programs of schools, hospitals, water and sewer, roads, many times picking up the responsibility of the Federal Government. That is coming through our gaming revenue. That is our essential revenue base. And we feel it is infringing upon our tax base if the United States or the States were to tax that revenue, because we are providing the essential revenue that is the basis for our community life.

The CHAIRMAN. Well, let me say, it is good to have you, Mark. And you are now the Senior Advisor.

Mr. VAN NORMAN. Thank you, Mr. Chairman.

Mr. STEVENS. If I could, Mr. Chairman, Mark's last day as a full-time employee is the 31st of December. As of this week, Mr. Jason Giles, our Deputy, has been promoted by the Executive Board. So Mark has been with us for 11 years, as Senior Advisor, it is a great responsibility as well. But I appreciate the acknowledgment. He has been of great service to the National Indian Gaming Association.

The CHAIRMAN. Thank you, Mr. Stevens.

Let me ask one more question, and I have other questions, but I am going to ask the Vice Chairman for his questions. This question is to Senator D'Amato. One of the concerns surrounding Tribal involvement in Internet gaming is that only a few Tribes may be able and ready to participate, should legislation be enacted. Are there ways you could envision a large number of Tribes being able to participate in Internet gaming?

Mr. D'AMATO. Yes, Mr. Chairman. As you correctly said, not only are there few Tribes who could move into this space within a relatively short period of time, but even the large brick and mortars, they are not all ready to move in. So there would be some time.

But by network partnering, as I mentioned, whether it is the Mohegans or the Oneidas or some of the other Tribes, who may or may not have their own Internet site, but by partnering, they become very powerful. And by affiliations, allowing others to come in and join and take a percentage, they don't even need to set up their own through their portal. They could get, for example, most people I have heard discuss it like 10 percent would be theirs for referring the people who use their site and then hook into the larger one.

And there is no doubt that this is the kind of thing that even the larger operators will be doing, offering affiliate programs to commercial entrepreneurs, non-Indian Tribes as well as Indian Tribes. I think you are going to see a cross-pollenization with people attempting to bring in as many as they can.

One of the reasons that State legislation doesn't work is because there are very few States who could get enough participants within their body. One of the reasons you need Federal legislation, by the way, is to keep the bad operators who are presently operating, not only poker sites, but sports betting. And you know, people are against kids getting hooked, well, right now you have no protection against them. You have dozens and dozens of offshore sites who are offering all kinds of games without any kind of supervision.

I just suggest that if we want to, some legislation that brings about good Federal oversight and certainly the fact of the matter is that the established system that today exists as it relates to regulating Indian gaming certainly can be utilized as it relates to their operations. But right now, the people basically in this Country are not protected. And if you want to stop illegal activities, then we have to regulate.

The CHAIRMAN. Thank you.

Senator Barrasso, your questions.

Senator BARRASSO. Thank you very much, Mr. Chairman. I think what we hear is that there is a significant loss of revenue going offshore; that there is a lack of consumer protection; that no Tribe should be required to go back and alter any compact with the State. We hear of the potential and the success of pooling together of Tribes. And that what is unfair today is possibly the lack of supervision. That is what I believe I have heard across the board here today.

Senator D'Amato, you had mentioned something about the Tribes polling together. Would this be a way to avoid a conflict of interest or also in terms of a regulatory standpoint? Where you are not just looking at yourself but others are helping in providing some of that fairness that you have described?

Mr. D'AMATO. It would have that dual effect. It would give to those Tribes, many of them simply don't have the resources to go out on their own, to be able to become full participants in this. Whereas they could never do it in and of themselves.

Secondly, they are much easier to regulate, if you have one group who is pooling, whatever the regulatory authority is, whether it is on the State basis or whether it is through the Indian gaming council, why then, much more effective as it relates to that supervision.

Senator BARRASSO. The other question, Senator D'Amato, is that you were going through a number of issues and ran out of time, as so often happens here. I just wonder if there is any additional overview or perspective that you would like to help offer to help clarify the big pictures.

Mr. D'AMATO. I would. And I hope that maybe this would put some spotlight, and by the way, I understand those concerns who say, by the way, you are affecting our business, our industry, we want to be part of this process, we want to know what is taking place. I think that is why we can and should be sitting down together to work out some of these details.

I think Mr. Gobin, the Vice Chairman, when he spoke, talked about what could potentially take place and destroy Indian gambling as we understand it. Well, let me say, there is a ticking time bomb, and it is not this legislation, which exists in State governments today. And no one has talked about that. And that is the lotteries in these States that now are considering what they call scratch-off. And these scratch-off games are nothing more, when you put them on the video, than guess what? The slot machine. And that is where most casinos make, and particularly Indian casinos as one of them, their large revenues.

Now, what takes place if, let's supposing, State X enacts this? One of the larger States, because they want to raise revenue. That will absolutely impact negatively what will take place in the brick and mortar casinos. So for their own protection, you need regulation that will say, not allowed. You need regulation that says, sports gambling, not allowed. You can't stop it today if it is coming from offshore. You can stop it if you have a Federal regulation.

So the ticking time bomb is here, and it is within the municipal operations. I am not going to be begin to start trying to name States, but there are States who are pursuing this now, they want to raise revenue. And it will be a great source of revenue to them.

Now, does the Federal Government have the ability to come in and stop them? I don't think so. I want to see what attorney general is going to sue a particular State and try to stop them. I don't think they are going to find such an easy time. Because the Wire Act does not control the Internet. It doesn't. And so there is that need, this necessity for Congress to take steps to regulate, to protect the consumers and to protect the very industry that everyone here is talking about, the Indian nations and the commercial brick and mortar operations as well.

Senator BARRASSO. Thank you. Thank you very much, Mr. Chairman.

Mr. VAN NORMAN. Mr. Chairman, if I might interject on those points just briefly?

I would say that Indian Country has been strongly involved with the Internet gaming debate for quite some time. Chairman Stevens has established an Internet Gaming Subcommittee. We have had very active meetings with Tribes across the Country.

We participated very actively in the development of the legislation that led to the Unlawful Internet Gambling Enforcement Act. And what we asked for was a fair regime. I have to say that there hasn't been a real strong effort up until 2010 to enforce that 2006 law. So you are still in sort of the beginning stages of that enforcement.

I think what Senator D'Amato is referencing is that there are many aspects of those laws that would be enforced even if you have a poker-only legislation that this other part of the law does need to have strong enforcement.

I would also say on the question of regulating versus operating for Indian Tribes, it goes to separation of powers. With Indian affairs, it is always important to remember history. The founding fathers visited the Iroquois Confederacy to find out about the principles of separation and powers in a divided government where responsibilities are given to different institutions.

Basically what we have in Indian Country is our Tribal regulatory agencies are separate and independent of our operations. It is not an offense to self-government to have that separation of powers. We honor that and we think we can do the same thing, as Chairman Bozsum was pointing out, with Internet gaming that we have done with Indian gaming. If you look at the capacity of some of our larger Tribes, I will just mention that the Mashantucket Pequot Tribe, in their security system, has more storage capacity than the Library of Congress. They helped the FBI track down a notable fugitive, Gotti, through their surveillance system. The Tribes have good systems in place. And that is part of our self-government.

The CHAIRMAN. Thank you very much, Mark Van Norman, for that response.

Thank you very much, Vice Chairman Barrasso.

Ms. Coleman, in your testimony, you emphasized that Tribes need to be able to opt in or opt out of Internet gaming, regardless of what the State does. Are there any precedents in Indian Country for this?

Ms. COLEMAN. Yes, there are, Chairman.

The CHAIRMAN. Since you spent that many years.

[Laughter.]

Ms. COLEMAN. I have spent a 30-year career in Indian law, and I have run into a few over the years. Probably the most interesting one, the one that recognizes to a large extent the different cultural values and the need to recognize the differences between States and Tribes is in legislation that allows Tribal nations to opt out of the death penalty in first degree murder cases. So they can choose to not have the death penalty imposed against their members.

And that seems like an extraordinarily important way of looking at things. The nations have these values that are not necessarily going to be reflected in the State.

And there is bigger legislation that does the same kinds of things, like the Indian Reorganization Act, Tribes could opt in or they could opt out. And many, like the Hodenoshone or the Navajo Nation, they didn't ascribe to the Federal Government's view of how their nations should be organized. And they have been the better for it.

And Public Law 280, which gives criminal jurisdiction to States, about six of the States, the criminal jurisdiction was mandated. But for most of the rest of the States, the States could ask for jurisdiction, criminal jurisdiction and the Tribes had to agree to giving the State criminal jurisdiction.

So those are the kinds of policy. Congressional policy over the years has always recognized those kinds of rights for Tribal nations.

The CHAIRMAN. Thank you very much.

Mr. Grant Eve, in your testimony you mentioned that the impacts of Internet gaming on traditional Indian gaming facilities will depend on whether Tribes are given equal footing in legislation. What do you think Tribes would need in legislation to be on equal footing?

Mr. EVE. Thank you for the question, Chairman. That is a hard question to ask, because the legislation, we really don't know, except for Congressman Barton's bill. But I think you go back to early entrance, everyone on equal playing fields and no one have early entrance. Then back to the separation of powers, where Tribes are a government and a sovereign nation and they have the regulatory arm, they can operate, regulate, hold everyone accountable. And then you have the operator arm as well, where those are the operators.

Because at the end of the day, you are still a hospitality industry and an entertainment industry. And if you can't provide your customer with reliance on the Internet site, then your operation is no good, if it falters. I think the Tribes have done a dang good job with that, and they have shown that with their past history.

The CHAIRMAN. Thank you very much, Mr. Eve.

Senator D'Amato, what is Poker Players Alliance's policy as it relates to Tribes participating in Internet gaming?

Mr. D'AMATO. They have to be given a seat at the same time as anybody else. They should not surrender any of their sovereign rights. They don't have to. They should not be required, as I mentioned before, to renegotiate their compacts.

As it relates to taxation, that begins to become a thorny issue, but one that can be solved. And we are not talking about onsite, we are talking about the customers it serves off of reservation. And as Chief Ernie has indicated, or Chairman Ernie has indicated, for example, they pay fees to be regulated. Their customers could then pay a fee to participate, whether it is 2 percent, 3 percent, whatever is worked out.

But these are things that can be done, protecting the sovereignty of the nation and not placing anyone, either the Indian nations or the commercial enterprises, at a disadvantage. The affiliation, giving them the ability to affiliate with both Indian Tribes and non-Indian Tribes, I could see some of the traditional brick and mortar non-Indian operations looking to bring Indian Tribes in as a way of gaining more players to come to their brick and mortar site as well as to play on the Internet. It is a win-win.

But one thing that is not a win is allowing the status quo to exist where there is literally no enforcement. If we want to prevent the people from sending in the signal, then you have to make it illegal. It is not illegal right now. The Wire Act, in which they are attempting to operate, doesn't cover it, to answer Mark's question. It does not. And the Circuit Court, the Third Circuit, said that, it spelled it out.

So why leave this very ambiguous situation where you do and can get shady operators coming in offshore, cannibalizing and taking business away? I don't know how much business they take away from the brick and mortars, as it relates not to poker, but as to other games.

And one last thing. The legislation we are supporting is not gambling. It comes down to one thing: poker only. So we are poker only specific. We are not talking about opening up, because if we were, I can assure you, Mr. Chairman, there would be many other representatives here. I don't think the brick and mortar industry would stand still, whether it came from New Jersey or whether it came from Las Vegas. They are not ready to permit full scale gambling, nor is the NFL, which was the group that pushed this legislation, the Internet Gambling Act, which is totally ineffective. Totally ineffective. It didn't protect the players when they are playing offshore. It's a canard.

So if we want to keep youngsters off the Internet, then let's regulate it. We can do that. If we want to see the people get a good game, then let's get a regulator in there that sees that it is fair and honest. If we want to see that the poker players' money is set aside in an escrow account so that it can't be utilized as we saw took place with full tilt, well, then, let's see that we have rules and regulations that require that. Then let's bring in the kind of people to regulate and who will see that these rule are enforced.

No action is the wrong thing. And the business is saying, I don't want my little kid playing, well, your little kid is playing on the Internet now without any supervision, without any regulation, with operators who may or may not be running a fair game. So my gosh, it really cries out. And to have people say, oh, no, you are going to entrap little kids, what do you think is happening now? That is exactly their plan, without any kind of supervision from the Feds.

Now, there is also something called parental responsibility. But absent that, we have an obligation, as we did in our liquor laws, to pass a law that says, you are not supposed to sell, and we will try to enforce to the best of our ability those laws, whether they are 18 years in some States or 21 years. That is what we have done.

But to just simply say, don't use the Internet for this purpose, you are making a mistake. You are opening it up and you really are doing a disservice to the American citizen and taxpayer and the tax base. Because there are revenues. I think revenues are secondary. I think consumer protection is first, to see that people get an honest game. And then if revenues can be derived, then fine, so be it.

Thank you, Mr. Chairman.

The CHAIRMAN. Thank you very much.

Mr. Pappas, do you have anything to add to that?

Mr. PAPPAS. Just to simply say that the Poker Players believes that Indian Country should be substantial players in the U.S.-regulated market. We encourage it and we hope that they could be federally-recognized licensing bodies as well as operators. We speak for consumers, so the more entrants in the marketplace, the better. We welcome Indian Country as a substantial player in the market.

The CHAIRMAN. Thank you very much.

Mr. VAN NORMAN. Mr. Chairman, if I might jump in there a little bit. We appreciate some of the statements that have been made by the Poker Players Alliance. And the understanding that is worthwhile for us to maintain our government to government relationship with the NIGC and use our existing regulatory systems, I think that is very important to our sovereignty.

As far as the taxation goes, what we are concerned about is that we are funding the schools, the hospitals, the essential community programs that we need to make the reservations a liveable homeland. And we don't want to see an impact of an overlay of Federal and State tax dollars on that. There has been a history in the Country that Tribal governments, under the Internal Revenue Code, are not considered income tax payers because we are governments. That is an important principle for us to maintain.

If there is a regulatory fee, we can pay for the services that are rendered to Indian Country from the NIGC based on regulation. But we are concerned about maintaining our government status.

So I think this has been a very positive dialogue and we can move forward. I think it is clear that State lotteries as government agencies are also going to want to come into the dialogue here, and they are going to want to assert their position in this dialogue. I see that they are not at the table today. But in the future, I am sure they will be.

There also, on the House side as well as the Senate side, there has been a need for the Department of Treasury and the Department of Commerce and the Department of Interior to come forward and explain what their situation is. I think if there was a strong statement to the National Indian Gaming Commission that there will be a Congressional mandate for you to play an appropriate role, then they will respond. They are kind of sitting back, waiting for something where the language is coming their way. They will respond to a Congressional mandate. They are a top-notch agency and they can do a good job to fulfill a Congressional mandate.

The CHAIRMAN. Thank you.

Let me ask NIGA and Chairman Ernie Stevens, and it is following up on these comments. What would NIGA like to see as the next steps in this conversation about Internet gaming?

Mr. STEVENS. I think, Mr. Chairman, that we would continue to be proactive, we would like to continue to monitor and do our best to make sure that we can analyze this and be a part of this. I assure you, Mr. Chairman, that Tribes, not just through our Internet Subcommittee, but Tribes throughout this Country, individual sovereign governments, have continued to analyze and build the knowledge of this industry.

We will never move without the appropriate safeguards and regulations. I have said this before, Mr. Chairman, in front of this Committee, that our community mandates that we protect our assets, protect our communities. So while we are trying to do our best to move our communities forward, to get them out of some of the struggles they have had over the years, we will never do it at the expense of a safe, sound, regulated business.

So this is just one business that we will continue to analyze. And we are going to continue to move forward, analyzing economic development opportunities, this being one of them. I think that the Internet Subcommittee again is well-attended, and a lot of Tribal leaders will continue to stay involved. We want to be on top of this. We don't want to move too fast or too slow. We want what is appropriate for Tribal governments, and that is what we will stand for.

The CHAIRMAN. Thank you very much for your response.

Ms. Penny Coleman, based on your prior experience at the NIGC, how do you answer those would say that NIGC does not have the staff, the resources or the expertise to regulate Internet gaming?

Ms. COLEMAN. I would say that they are the only Federal agency that is even close. While they are not regulating Internet gaming, they are regulating wide area progressives, gaming that is done through the Internet tunnels rather than the bigger Internet. They are the ones that have a knowledge of gaming. They have a knowledge of Tribal nations. They already have the infrastructure in places, they have the regional offices. They are the ones that have the expertise, they are the ones that have the knowledge base. They can hire someone who has spent time regulating Internet gaming. And I think they are the ones who are going to be able to hit the ground running when it comes to regulation of Internet gaming.

The CHAIRMAN. Thank you very much, Ms. Coleman.

At this time, I want to provide you with an opportunity as a panel to make any final remarks you want to make about the conversations that have been going on, or something that you wanted to say and you didn't have time to say. So let me call on, I am going to start from the other end of the table, Mr. Grant Eve, for any comments, final comments you may have.

Mr. EVE. Thank you, Chairman. Being a certified public accountant, numbers jump out at me. That is what I look at. I hear the number of $40 billion provided to the Federal Government, and you mentioned looking for funds at the beginning of this hearing.

I think if you are looking at a poker-only bill, you really need to examine those numbers. Poker, I have studied the European financial statements and poker has slightly decreased on the publicly-traded ones, because that is all you can look at, all that is public knowledge. But you have seen poker slightly decrease and you have seen casino games increase exponentially. Those are higher margin games which would mean more revenue to the Federal Government if it was legalized in that bill.

So I would closely examine that $40 billion figure and where that comes from.

The CHAIRMAN. Thank you. Ms. Coleman?

Ms. COLEMAN. Just one last thought. In case there is any suggestion that one of these many bills that are floating around there, somebody wants to pass them, there are so many things in them that haven't been vetted, that need to be vetted, that even the authors I am sure never really thought about. For instance, none of the bills prohibit cyber cafes. So there are, it is possible to end up with cyber cafes in direct competition with the brick and mortars.

Those kinds of issues are rampant throughout all of the bills. And so we really would need to narrow it down and be able to go through each line, everybody have an opportunity to point out what the issues are, so that real policy decisions can be made before any legislation is ever passed.

The CHAIRMAN. Thank you very much.

Senator D'Amato?

Mr. D'AMATO. Mr. Chairman, first of all, let me tell you what a great delight and pleasure it was to be back here with you. I want to thank the panel and the previous panels. I think a lot of good, constructive suggestions have come forth.

I want to point out one little thing, though. Penny Coleman, your wealth of knowledge, I think as it relates to NIGC, being one of the enforcement arms and licensing arms for the Tribe, for the Tribes in particular, certainly that is something that can and should be considered and I think undertaken with the proper staffing. And I agree as it relates to the Internet expertise, you can bring them in with a degree of relative ease. Everyone who gets into this will have to have the same problems. But they certainly have the capacity to undertake that and States will undoubtedly license some and provide for regulation, as they would.

There would be, and no one touched on this, I didn't touch on it, an opt-out provision so that if you had a State that did not want to, it could opt out of, and there probably are several States who would choose to do so.

Last but not least, the cyber cafes in at least one of the bills is clearly prohibited. And if we were again to go into poker only, I think it provides a needed protection that does not exist. Again, this is not going to be easy.

But I think if we work in a constructive way that Chairman Stevens has suggested and that others have suggested, I think that we can produce within a relatively short period of time a good, comprehensive bill that does what I think the IGA people thought they were going to accomplish but have not accomplished. And that is to get rid of some of the abuses that exist today, the youngsters who come on with no supervision, the problem gamblers. There are things that can be done to deal with that and to protect the consumers.

And again, there is no way that we are talking about anything other than at this time, and I have to agree with Grant, the revenue projections as it relates to poker only will be a lot less than what has ben predicted. But they will be substantial. I guess it was Everett McKinley Dirksen who said, a billion here and a billion there, and before you know it, we have quite a bit of money. So it will produce some monies.

Thank you, Mr. Chairman.

The CHAIRMAN. Thank you very much, Senator.

Chairman Stevens, please.

Mr. STEVENS. Mr. Chairman, I would just like to read this last statement I made. If Congress is going to change the system, Tribes as that new law follow these principles, and it provide a fair access to Tribes, that it continue to treat Tribes as government, and that it respect the essential government purposes for which Tribal revenue is used. Respect for Tribal governments and helping us to promote economic development, we are working on this, we are monitoring this.

It is not Ernie Stevens, it is not Mark Van Norman. It is the Tribal leaders, some of which are here today, from throughout this whole Country, are working hard on this. We are working hard on behalf of our community and our future. That is the bottom line.

We look forward to working with your team here, with your staff. We want to do a good job. And again, we want to provide for our children. Remember I told you at the beginning, I have 10 grandchildren. And those are the ones that we are responsible to, and that is why we want to do it and do it right. That is why the Internet Subcommittee, because of their leadership throughout this process, the Tribal leaders from throughout this Country are the ones we are counting on to lead us into this new era.

So if I could, I have to impose on you, Mr. Chairman, but I don't think this is the last time that Mr. Van Norman will be coming before you. I hope not. But certainly as a full-time employee of the National Indian Gaming Association, it will be. If I could just ask him to conclude our comments on behalf of the National Indian Gaming Association.

The CHAIRMAN. Please do, yes.

Mr. STEVENS. Thank you, Mr. Chairman.

The CHAIRMAN. Mr. Mark Van Norman.

Mr. VAN NORMAN. Mr. Chairman, we want to thank you for your leadership. This is a very important issue for Indian Country. We know you have already been looking at the infrastructure. We need help from the FCC on infrastructure. We need help from USDA, Department of Energy to put in the right infrastructure.

You may have recently seen on ABC the Diane Sawyer show about Pine Ridge. It talked about the deep unemployment, the terrible problems with alcohol abuse, the highway deaths of young people with young children that were caused by alcohol abuse. And the bright spot in that program was one of the mothers had an opportunity to go and work at the Indian gaming facility there at Pine Ridge. And they are not generating a lot of money.

But they are creating jobs and they are creating hope. And that is what Indian gaming means to us. And that is why it is so essential for us to be part of Internet gaming as it moves forward. And we appreciate the opportunity for dialogue and understanding of other folks that we have heard today. Thank you, Mr. Chairman.

The CHAIRMAN. Thank you.

Thank you very much. Again, I want to express my mahalo nui loa to all of you witnesses in today's hearing. The testimony we have heard today makes it clear that this is a very complex issue. And I feel that we have just scratched the surface of the issues here today and I know there were many other Tribes and other affected stakeholders that we need to hear from them as well.

That is why I intend to convene additional meetings about this issue, so my colleagues and I can make sure we are hearing from all interested parties and representing Tribal issues in this important matter. Your responses today have really moved us in that direction, and we will continue to work on it. Of course, the whole reason for all of this is to try to come to legislation, finally, if that will be in the best interest of all concerned.

So that is our goal, and I am glad to be part of it. I look forward to working with you on this. So thank you again very much. This hearing is adjourned.

[Whereupon, at 3:23 p.m., the Committee was adjourned].

APPENDIX

PREPARED STATEMENT OF HON. MARGIE MEJIA, CHAIRWOMAN, LYTTON RANCHERIA

Thank you for the opportunity to comment on the debate surrounding internet gaming. It is important for Congress to understand as it debates internet gaming issues that tribes are well positioned to be internet gaming operators and regulators if given a fair chance to compete. We are concerned that the discussion thus far is tilted in way that would disadvantage tribes who want to participate in internet gaming. There are those who suggest, out of self interest, that tribes are not ready to operate or regulate internet gaming. However, the history of tribal gaming demonstrates that this position is simply wrong.

Tribes have been engaging in various forms of gaming since long before the arrival of Europeans in North America. When the Indian Gaming Regulatory Act (PL 100-497, IGRA) was signed in to law on October 17, 1988, a strict new legal and regulatory framework was created for tribal gaming. IGRA created the National Indian Gaming Commission (NIGC) as the federal regulatory body to oversee tribal gaming. It also delineated three classes of games: Class I (social and traditional games), Class II (bingo and non-banked card games like poker) and Class III (other games such as banked card games and slot machines), with a specific regulatory structure for each class of games.

Since the enactment of IGRA, tribes operating under the provisions of IGRA, NIGC regulations, NIGC-approved tribal gaming ordinances, tribal-state compacts and the regulations of individual tribal gaming commissions have become experienced regulators *and* operators of sophisticated gaming operations. As many have indicated in testimony before this Committee, tribal gaming is the most highly regulated gaming activity in the United States.

For example, the Lytton Rancheria operates a successful Class II gaming operation in San Pablo, California. The Tribe operates a variety of card games, including various types of poker. The Tribe also offers over 1,300 Class II bingo terminals. We have top quality management and service staff and retain a robust and highly trained IT and data security team. We also have an experienced tribal gaming regulatory authority that regulates and monitors the Tribe's gaming operations.

Tribes such as Lytton have been innovators in the gaming industry and are well positioned to operate and regulate games offered via the internet. For example, tribes pioneered server-based gaming systems, which use many of the same technologies applicable to internet gaming. Similarly, tribes have adopted technologies that allow them to link games between reservations. Further, tribes were among the first to introduce cashless game systems which enable players to seamlessly move from machine to machine, taking their winning balances with them and only cashing out at the end of their play. Other tribal innovations include partnering with web development companies to offer "free play" poker and other casino games. Tribes continue to explore social media and new media to reach out to our customers.

Every day, tribes such as Lytton manage the operation of thousands of sophisticated gaming machines and process thousands of transactions and millions of dollars while safeguarding severs, databases and player information. These complex operations require the robust IT and data security teams which tribes currently train and employ. Moreover, tribes such as Lytton employ a host of accountants, attorneys, administrative staff, and marketing staff, many of whom have experience that would be directly relevant to operating and regulating an internet gaming site.

In short, tribes have the experience necessary to both operate and regulate internet gaming. There is no basis to treat tribes as less capable than commercial gaming interests in Nevada and New Jersey.

Conclusion

Tribal gaming operations are located throughout the nation in both large and small venues and account for nearly 40 percent of national gaming revenues. Additionally, tribes operate in a significantly more regulated legal environment than most non-tribal casinos. Tribes are technologically innovative, employ best practices for data security and are at the forefront of the development of new gaming technologies. As such, tribes have the experience necessary to fully participate in the operation and regulation of internet gaming. Congress should reject any attempt to cut tribes out of the emerging internet gaming market as it considers federal internet gaming legislation.

Thank you for your consideration.

58